Memories of Daughters

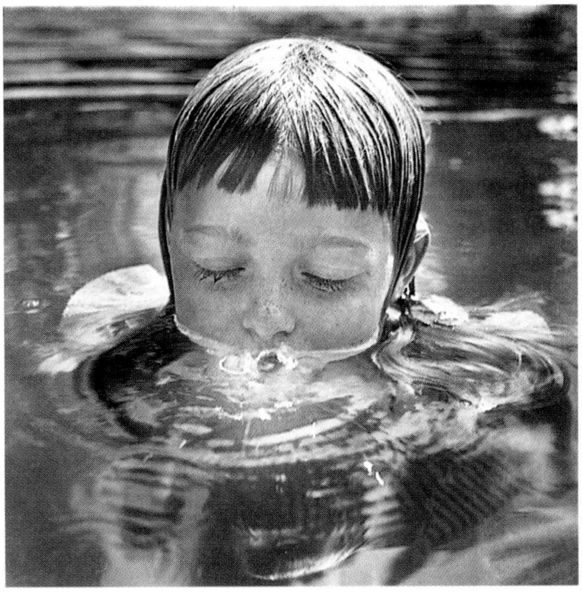

A GLORYA HALE BOOK
This 1996 edition is published by Park Lane Press,
a division of Random House Value Publishing, Inc.,
40 Engelhard Avenue, Avenel, New Jersey 07001.

Random House
New York • Toronto • London • Sydney • Auckland

Book and jacket design by Kathryn Wolgast Plosica

Printed and bound in the United States of America

Library of Congress Cataloging-in-Publication Data
Young, Myriam.
Memories of daughters / photographs by Myriam Young.
p. cm.
ISBN 0–517–20069–4
1. Girls—Portraits. 2. Young, Myriam.
3. Innocence (Psychology) in literature. I. Title.
TR681.G5Y68 1996
779'.25'092—dc20 95-17769
CIP
Rev.

8 7 6 5 4 3 2 1

Memories of Daughters

PHOTOGRAPHS BY MYRIAM YOUNG

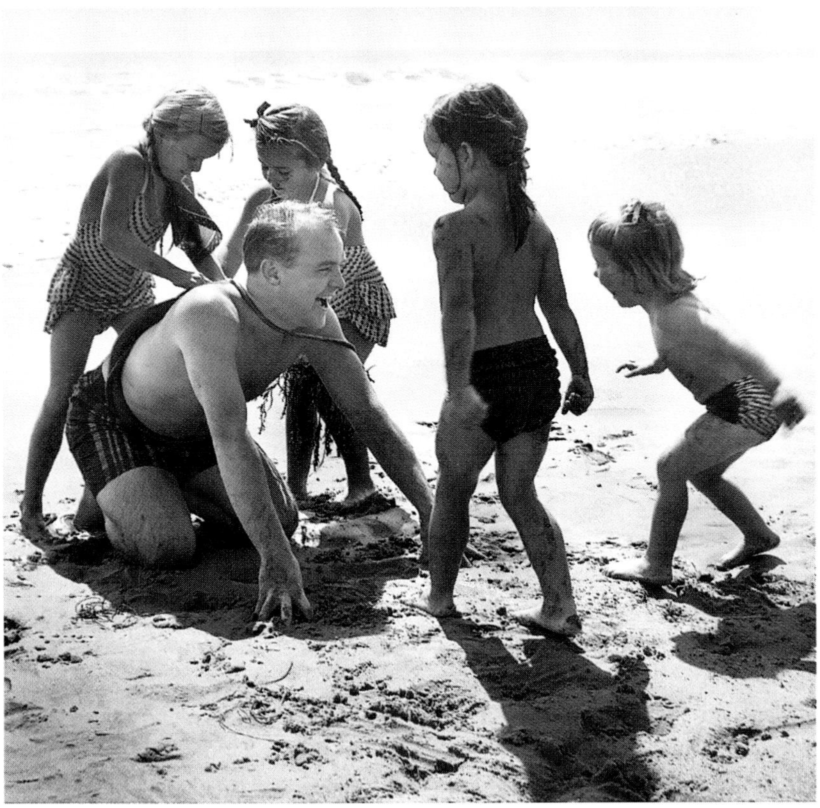

PARK LANE PRESS

New York • Avenel

To the spirits of the book—
Lisa, Kate, Theo and Abby, and Lorna

One day after the last of our four children was born, I knew I had to learn to photograph so I could make this book. I bought a camera, packed a suitcase with a few costume changes and took everyone on location for the weekend. I won a national prize with one of the pictures and spent the money on lessons with Ansel Adams. I used to come home in tears, struggling with Kelvin temperatures, zones, exposures and related wisdom, but the four beautiful spirits sustained me and let me try to catch them in my net as they flew by.

Out of those photographs I have chosen scenes and accompanying poem fragments that remind me of a time when we understood the language of birds, a time when things were magical, when magic had power, when dreams were real.

Each pairing of picture and poem is a meditation, for the child has the key and leads us to the hidden original heart of it all.

MYRIAM YOUNG

San Francisco
1996

Stand before it and there is no beginning.

Follow it and there is no end.

LAO-TZU

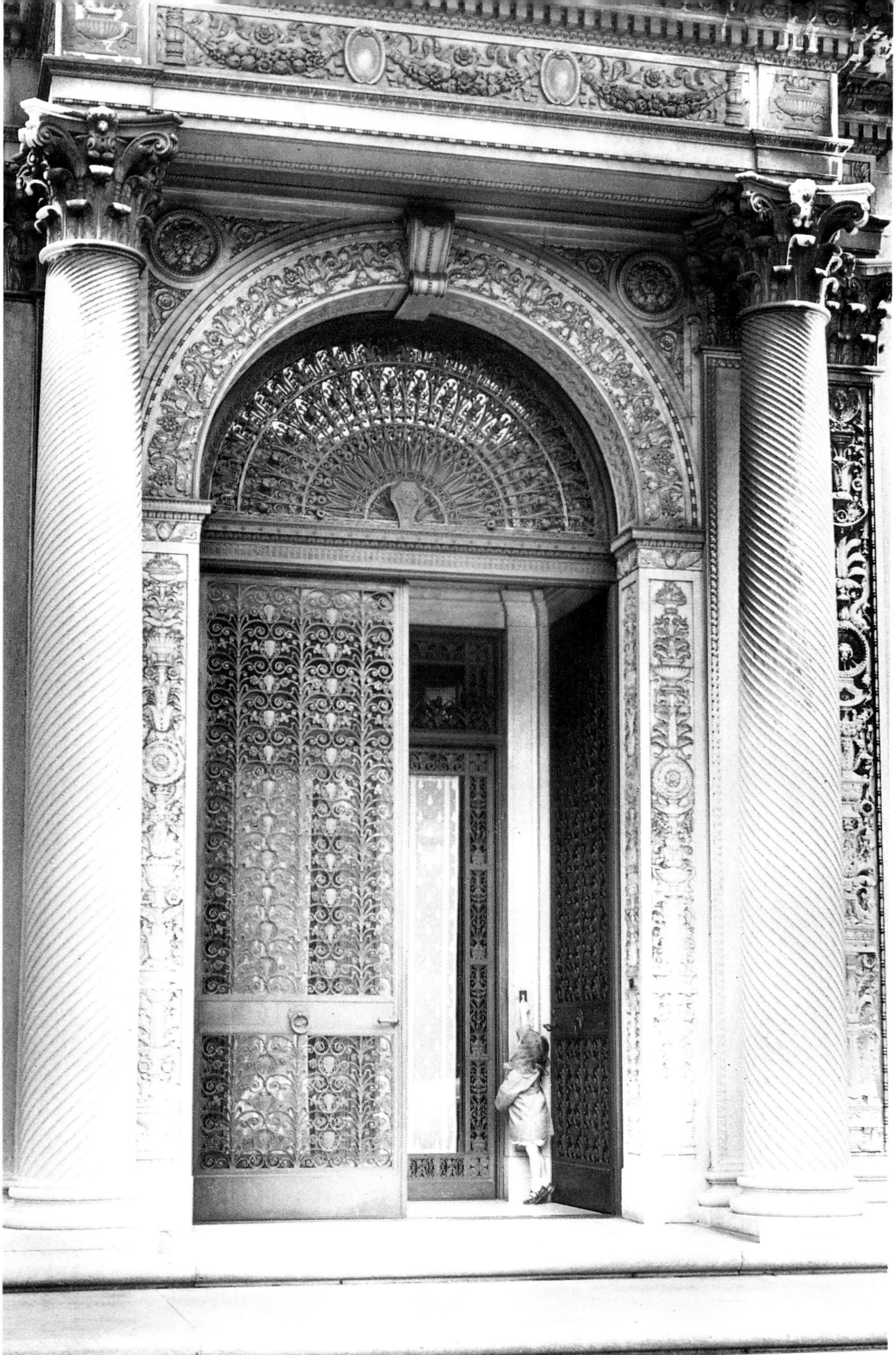

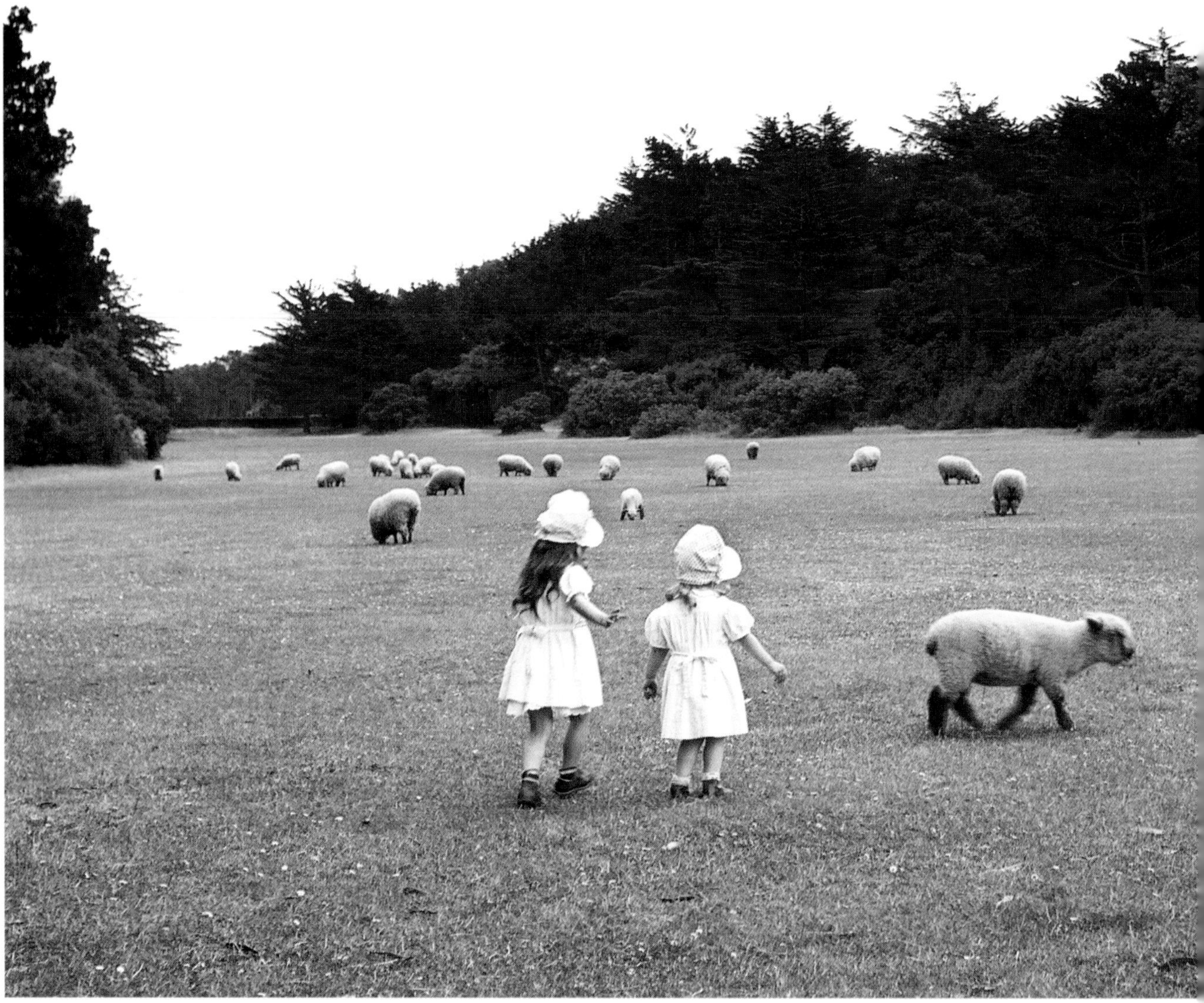

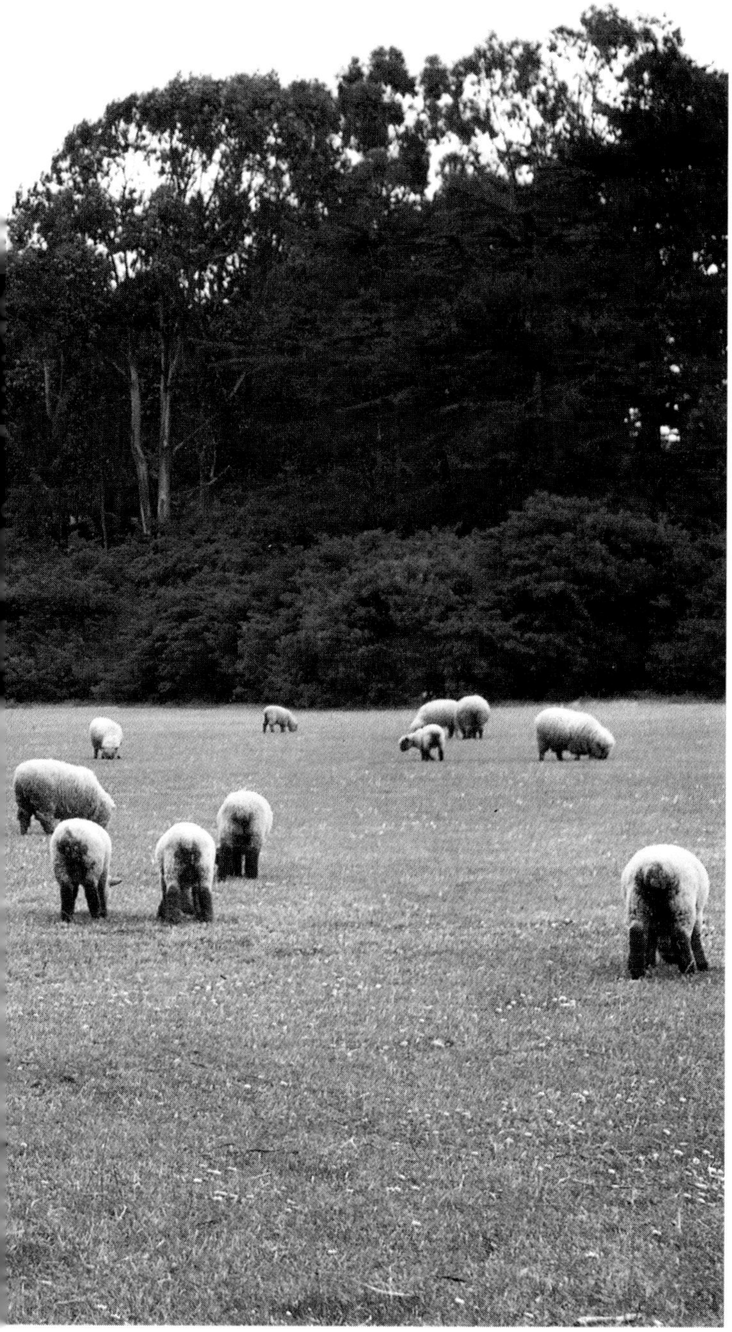

We were as twinn'd lambs that
did frisk i' the sun,
And bleat the one at the other:
what we chang'd
Was innocence for innocence.

WILLIAM SHAKESPEARE

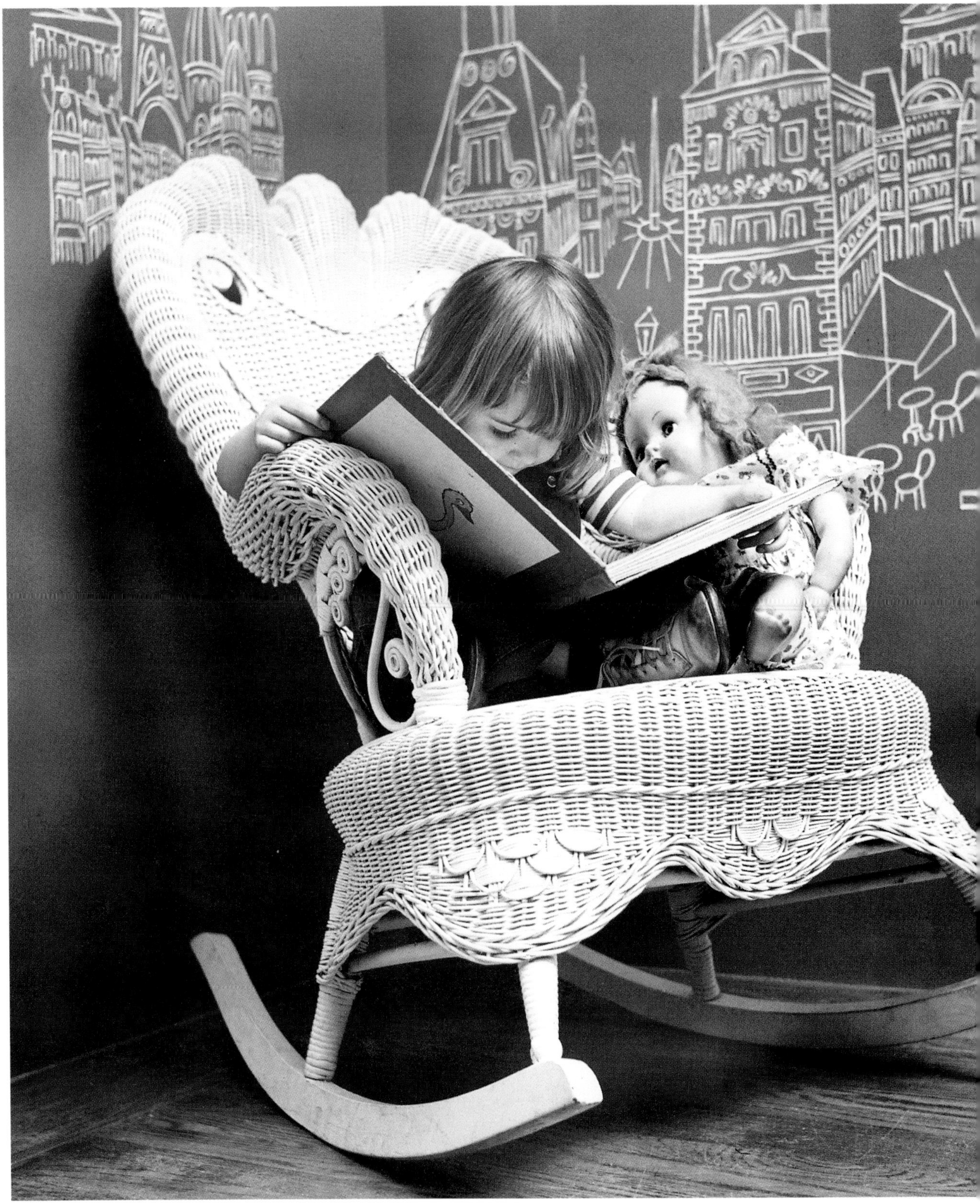

Are you aware how easy bygone things
become when you have lived a while,
how they prepare you quietly for wonders,
companion every feeling with a picture . . .

RAINER MARIA RILKE

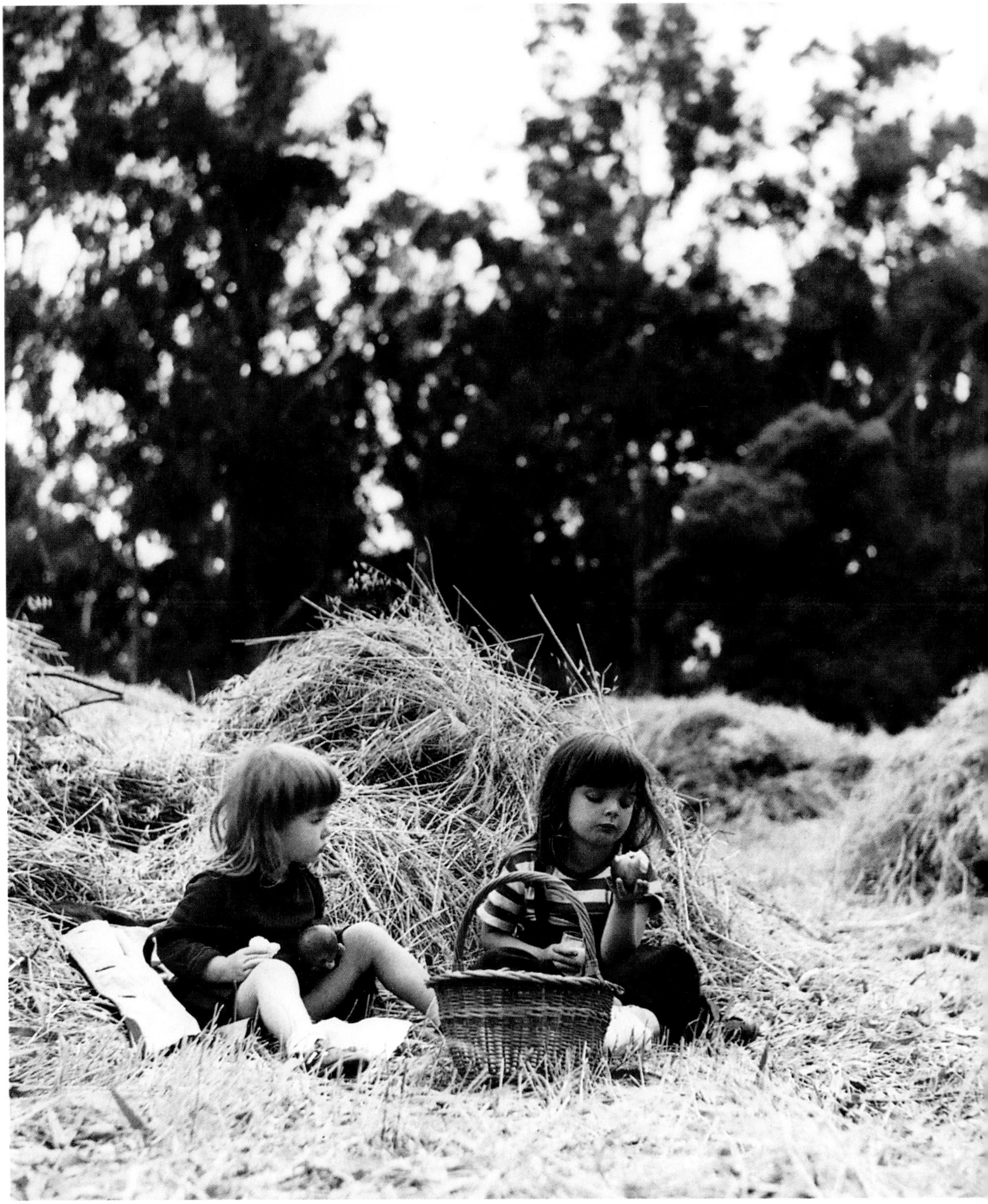

Oh Sacrament of summer days,
Oh Last Communion in the Haze—
Permit a child to join.
Thy sacred emblems to partake—
Thy consecrated bread to take
And thine immortal wine!

EMILY DICKINSON

I know not what my secret is,

I only know 'tis mine. . . .

ANDREW LANG

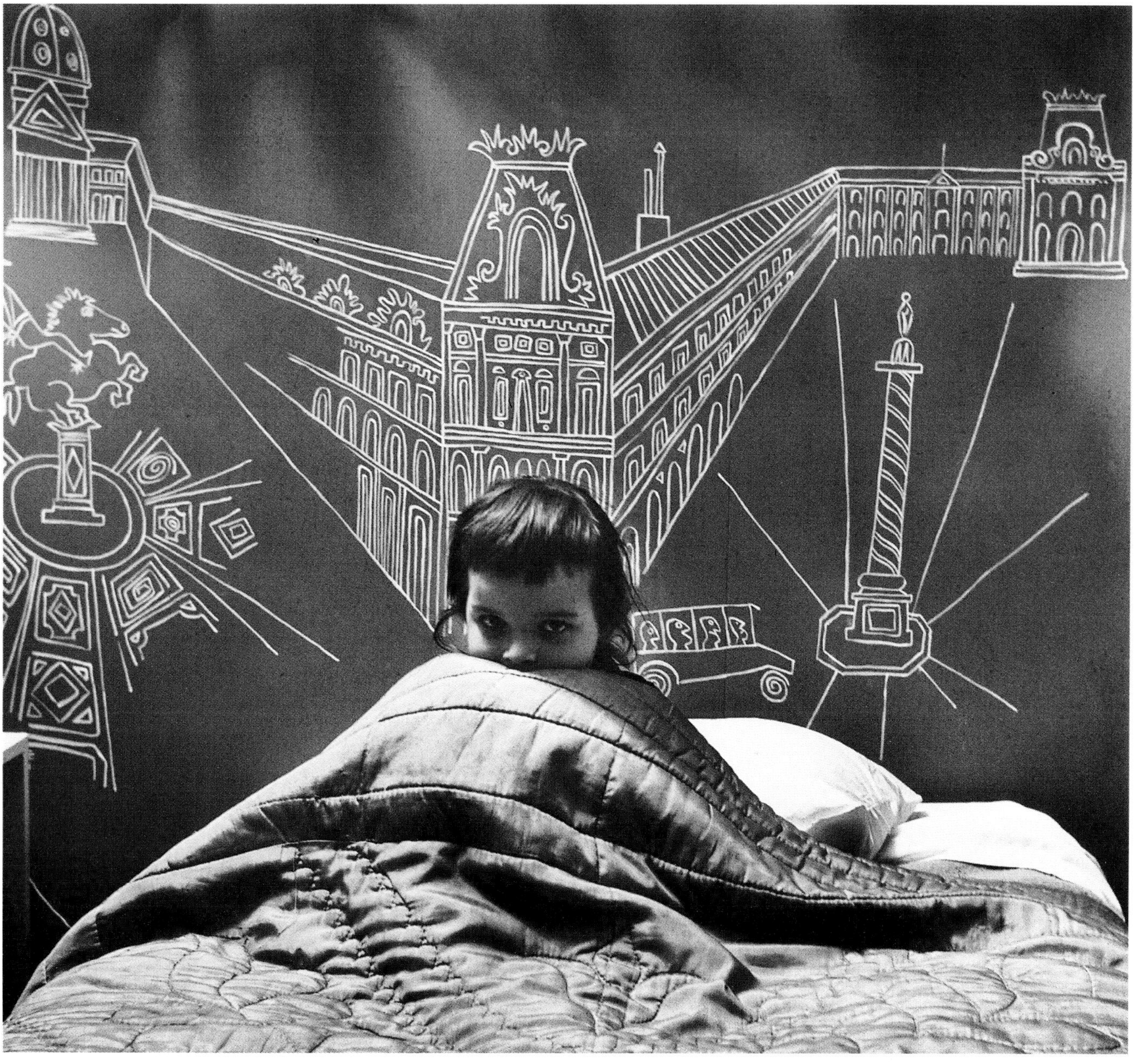

may my heart always be open to little
birds who are the secrets of living. . .

e. e. cummings

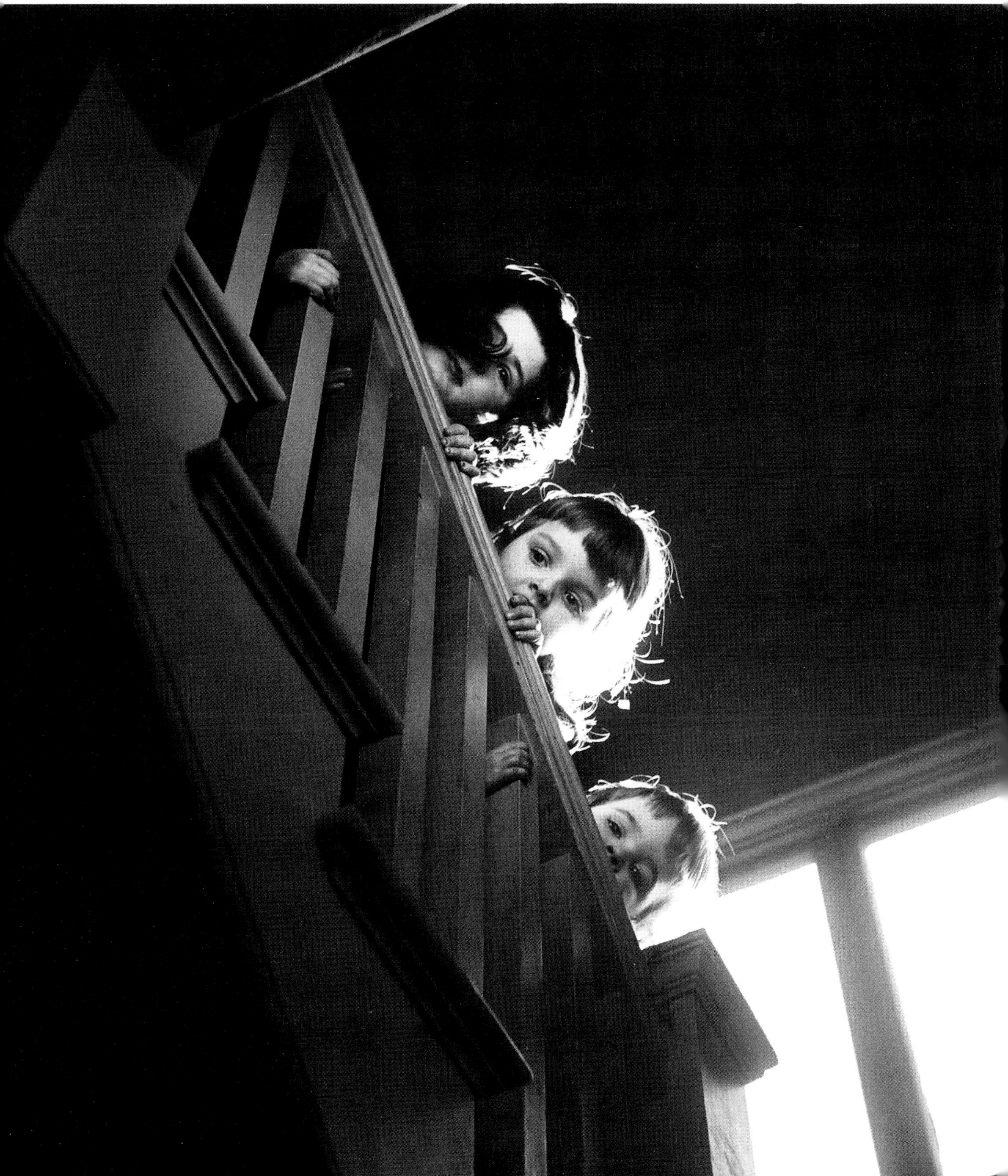

give back to me

my old soul,

the one I had as a child,

ripened by legends,

with its cap of feathers

and its wooden sword.

FEDERICO GARCÍA LORCA

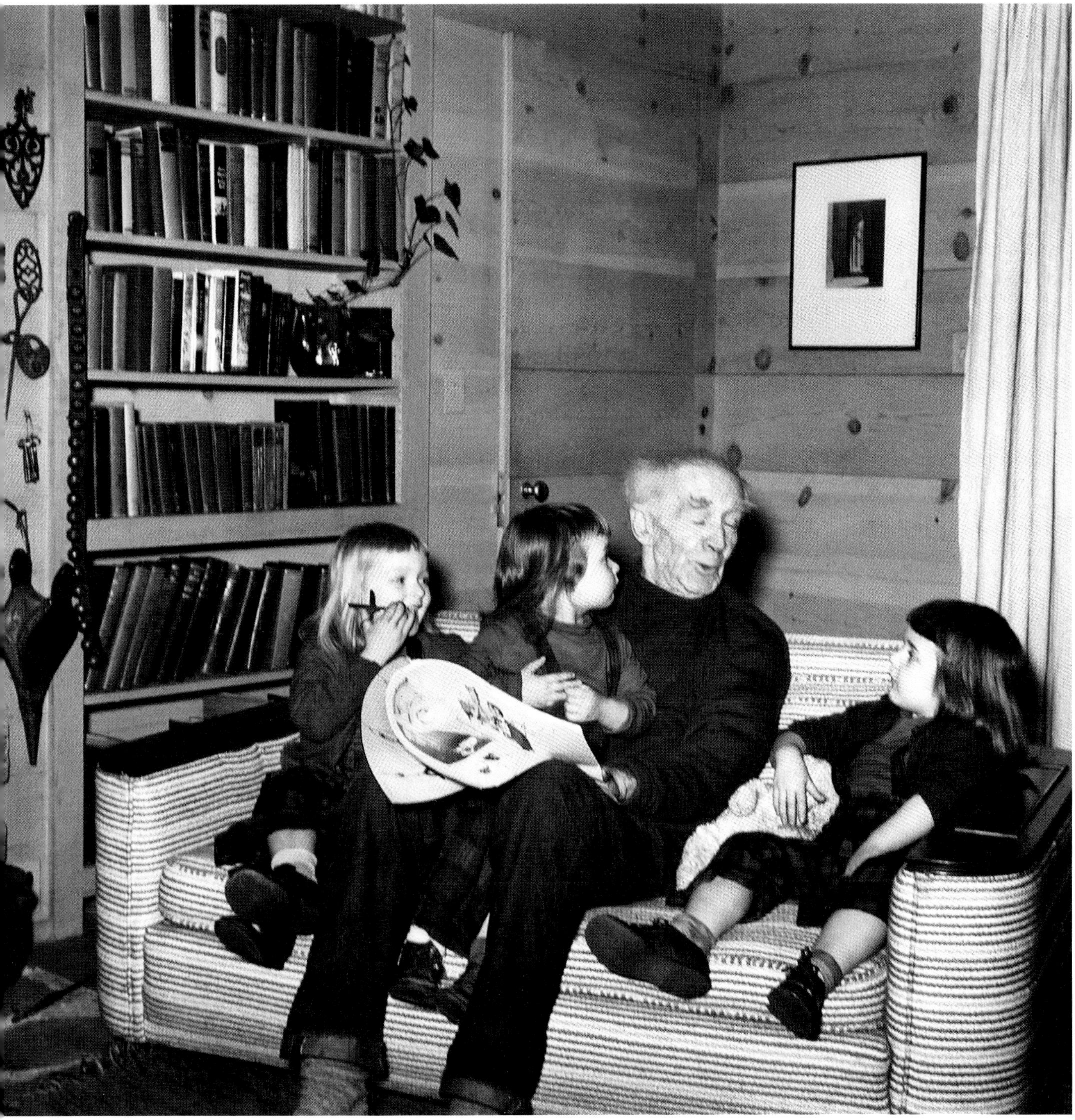

. . . a mind that is capable of looking without any distortion,
a mind innocent and vulnerable . . .

JIDDU KRISHNAMURTI

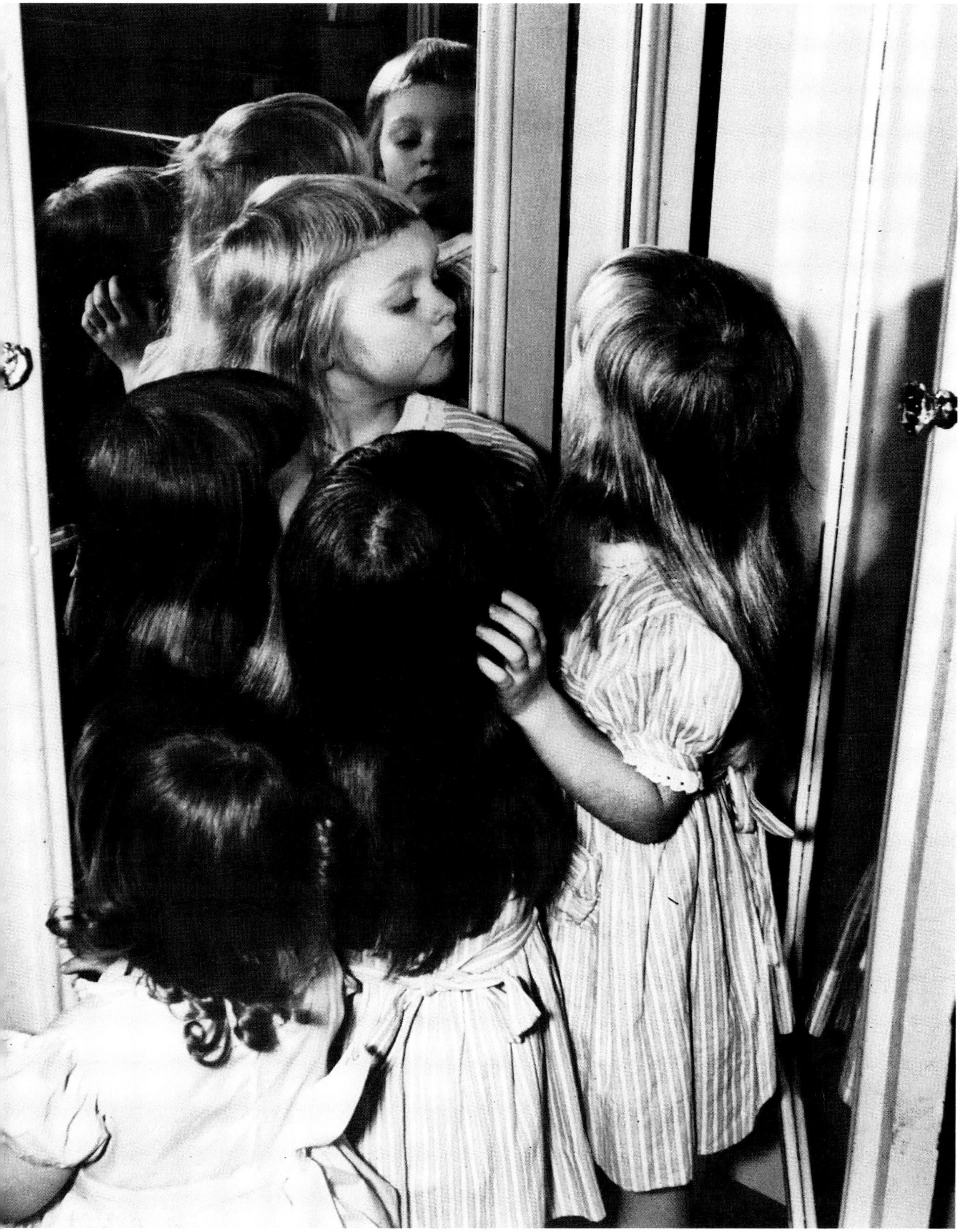

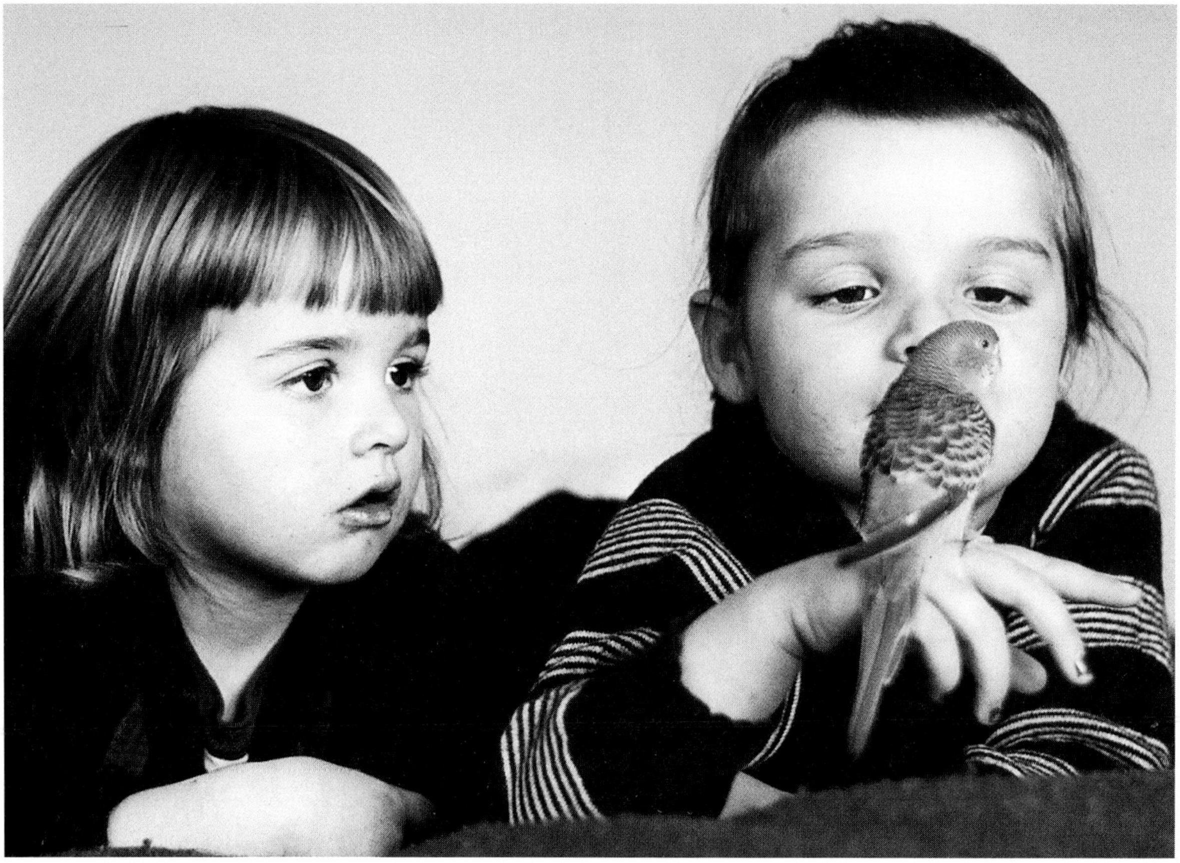

My heart takes wing in singing,
Under the trees of the forest,
The forest our dwelling and
our mother.
On my thread I have taken,
A little, a very little bird.
My heart is caught on the thread,
On the thread with the bird.

A PYGMY SONG

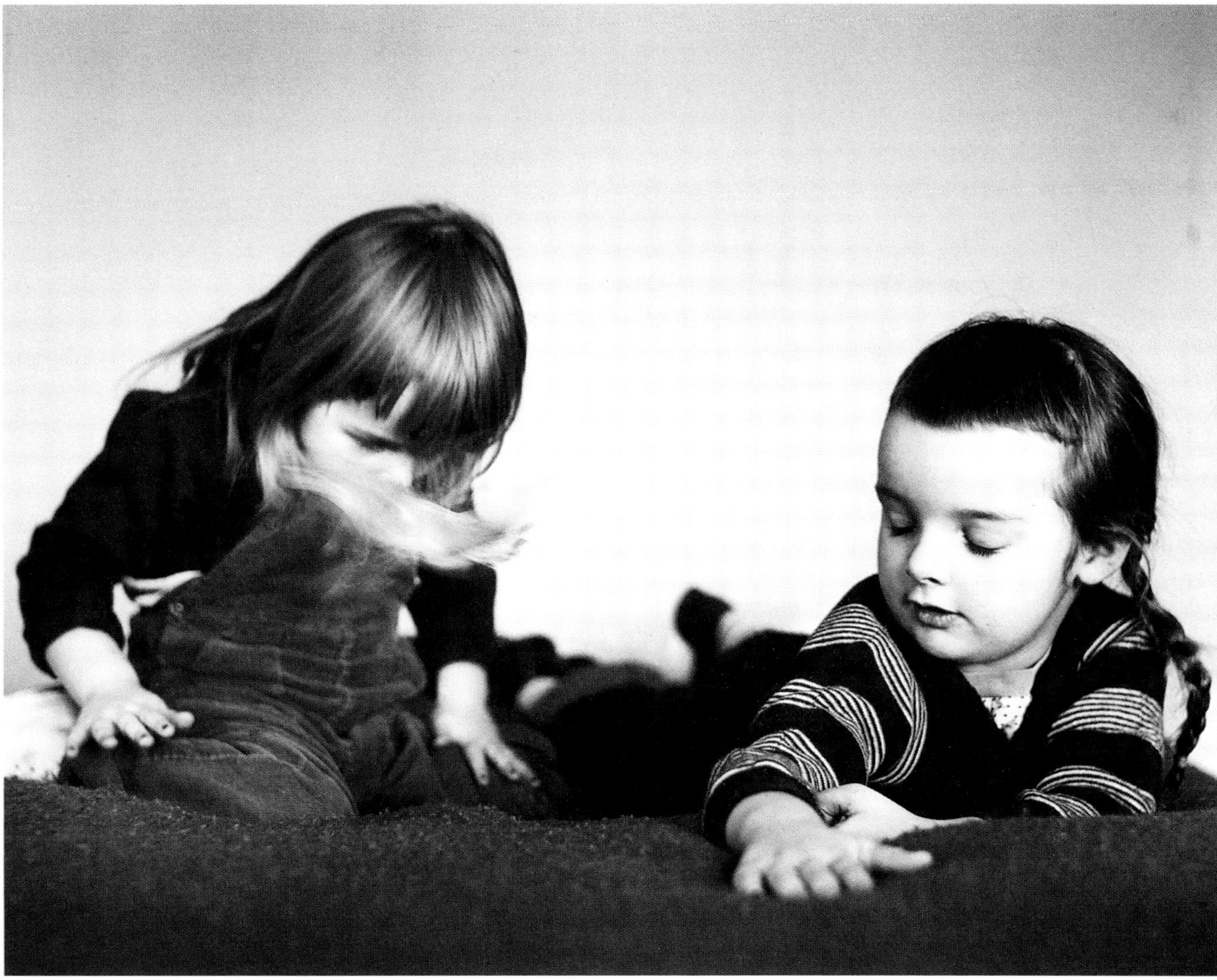

I celebrate myself, and sing myself. . .

WALT WHITMAN

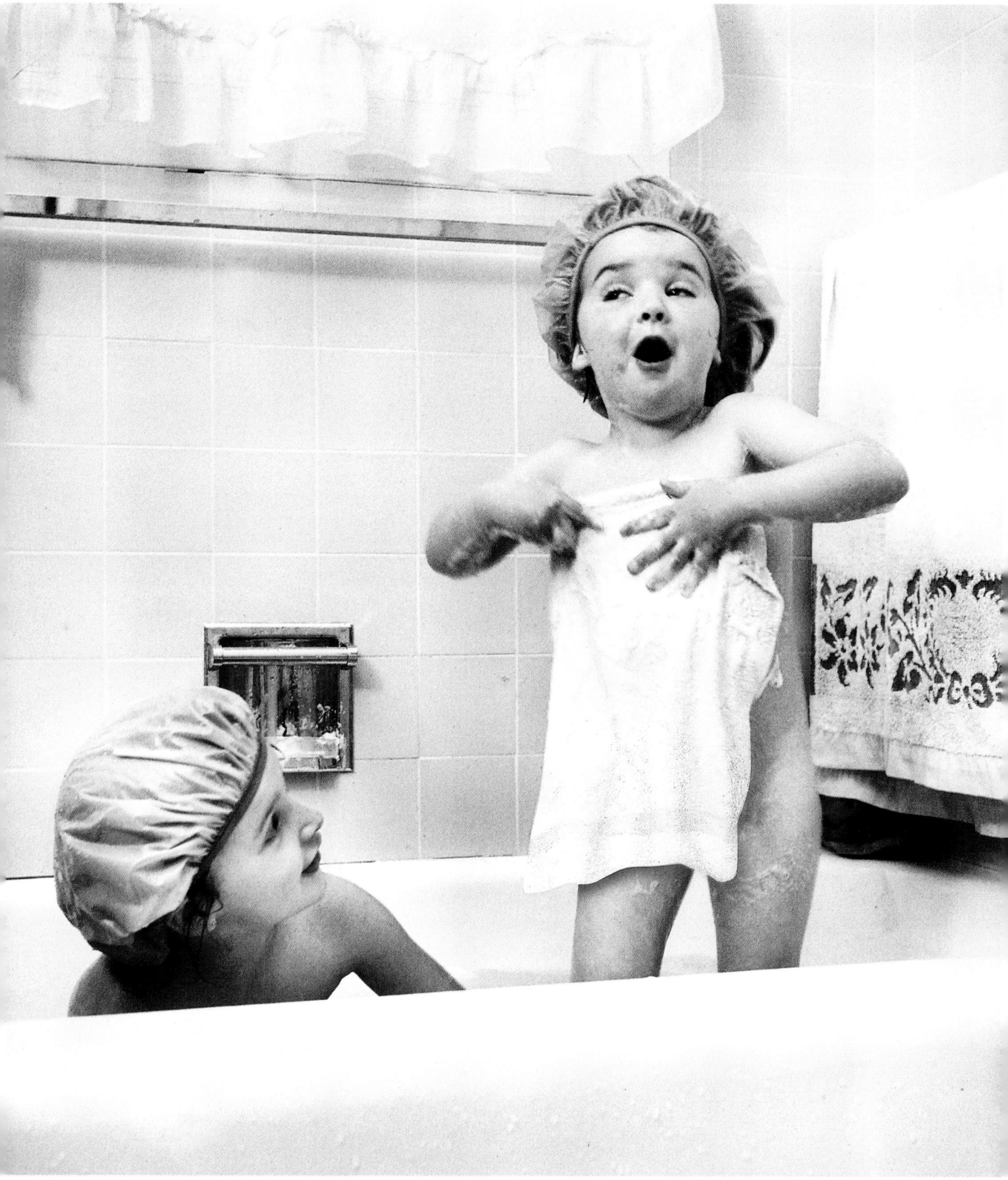

Like a great storm
the two of us shake
the tree of life
down to the most hidden
fibers of its roots
and you appear now,
singing in the leaves,
on the highest branch. . .

PABLO NERUDA

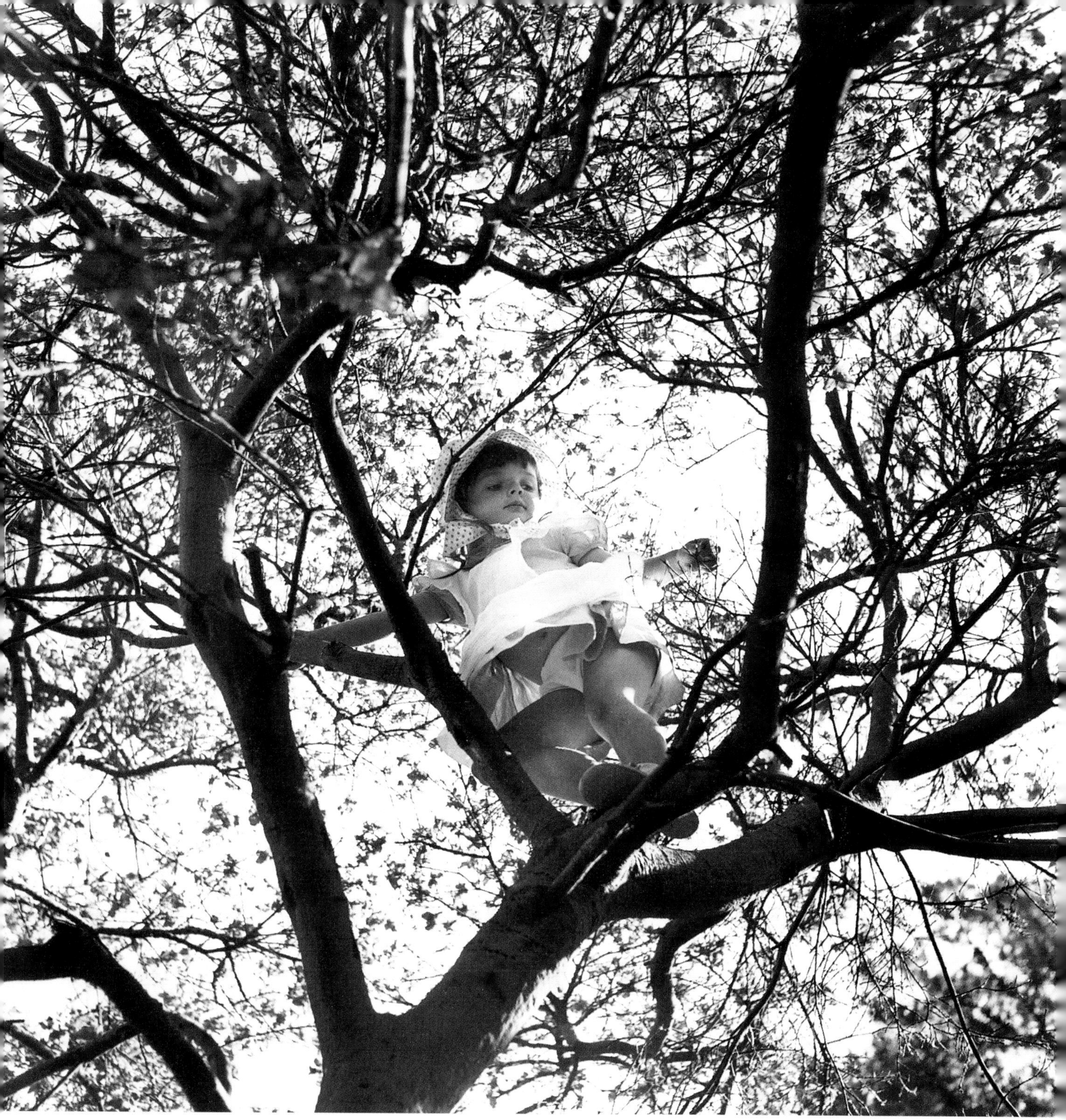

All creatures flourish together,
content with the way they are,
endlessly repeating themselves,
endlessly renewed.

LAO-TZU

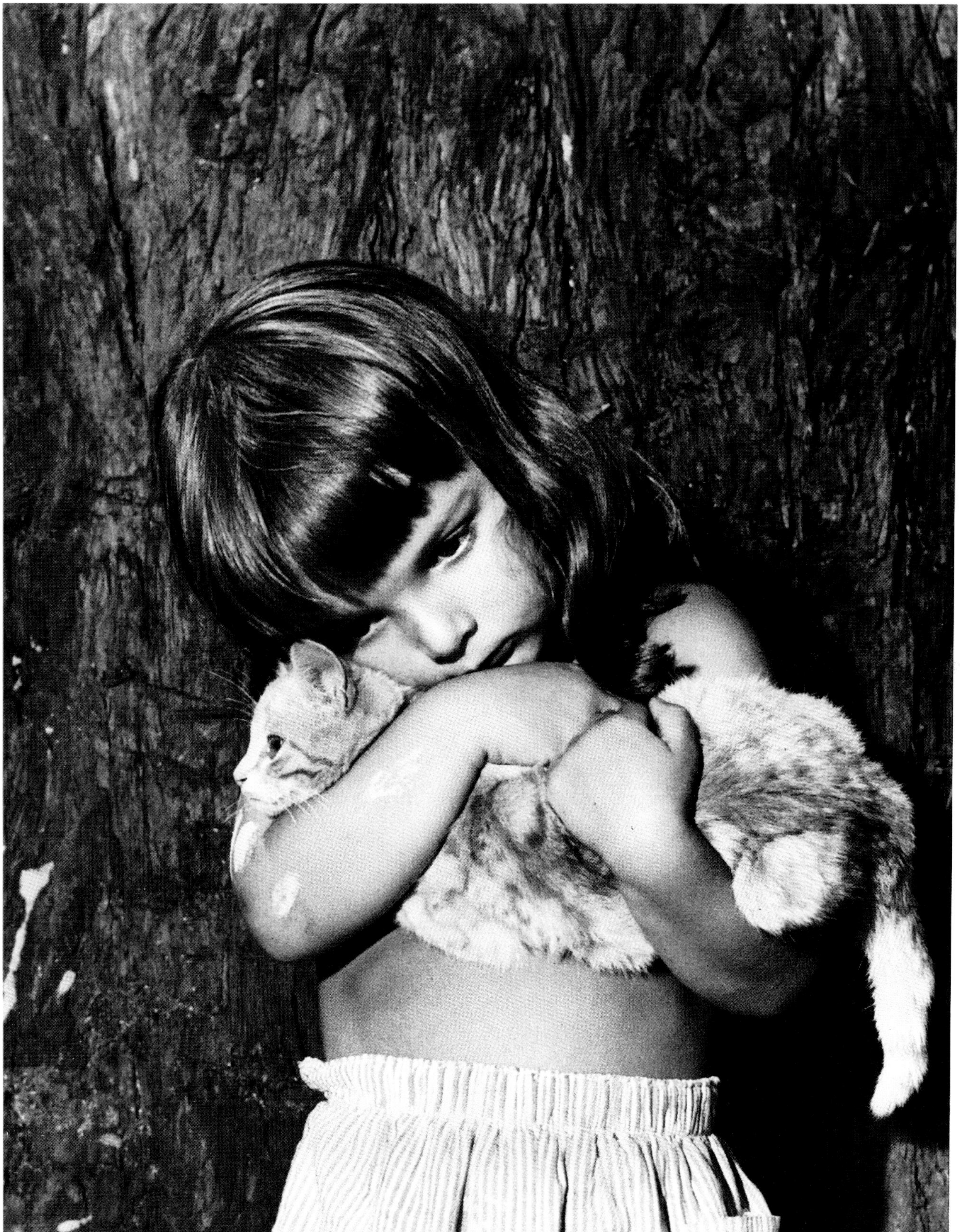

Up the airy mountain,
Down the rushy glen,
We daren't go a-hunting
For fear of little men;
Wee folk, good folk,
Trooping all together;
Green jacket, red cap,
And white owl's feather.

WILLIAM ALLINGHAM

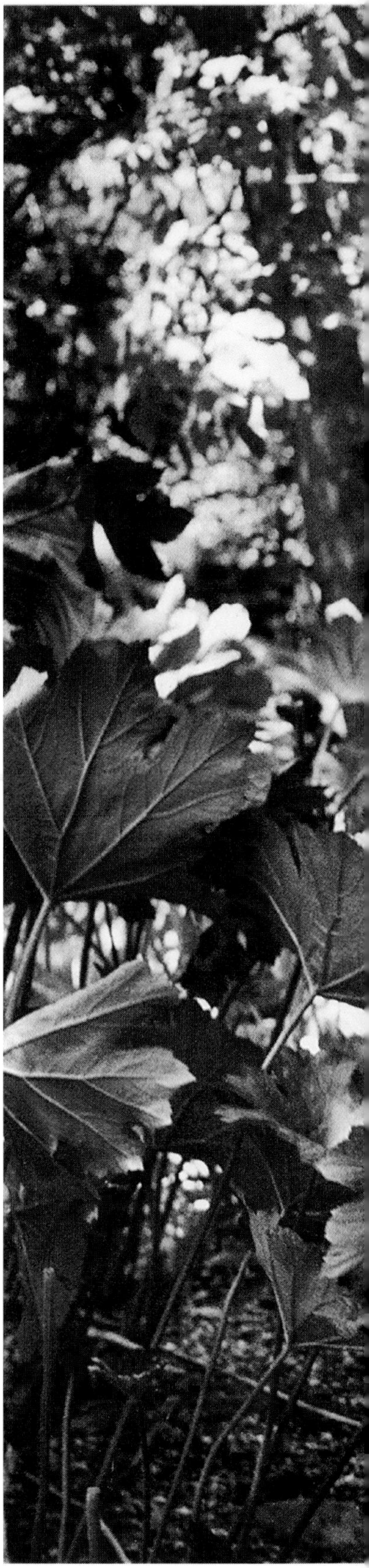

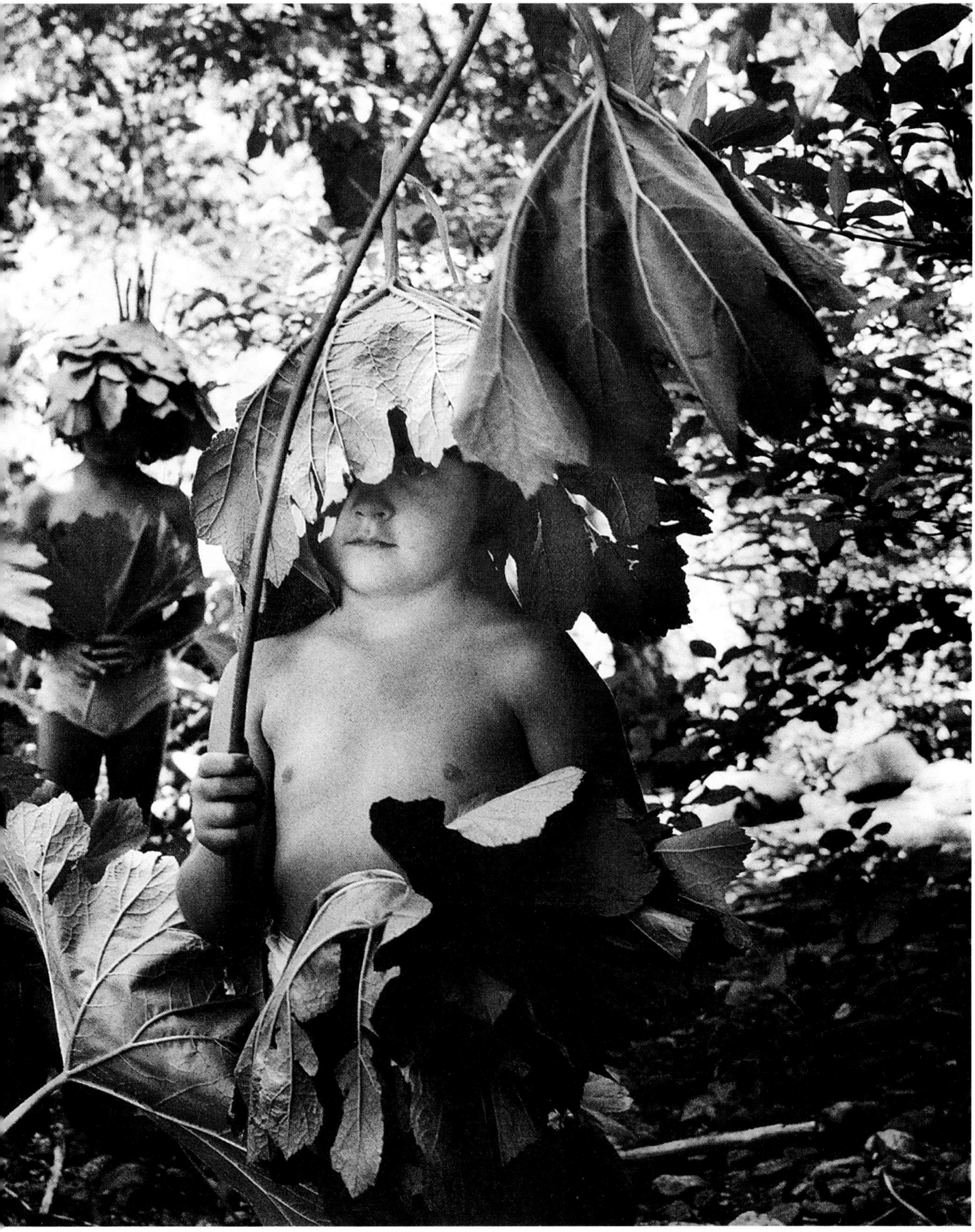

The Fairies have never a penny to spend,
They haven't a thing put by,
But theirs is the dower of bird and of flower
And theirs are the earth and sky.

ROSE FYLEMAN

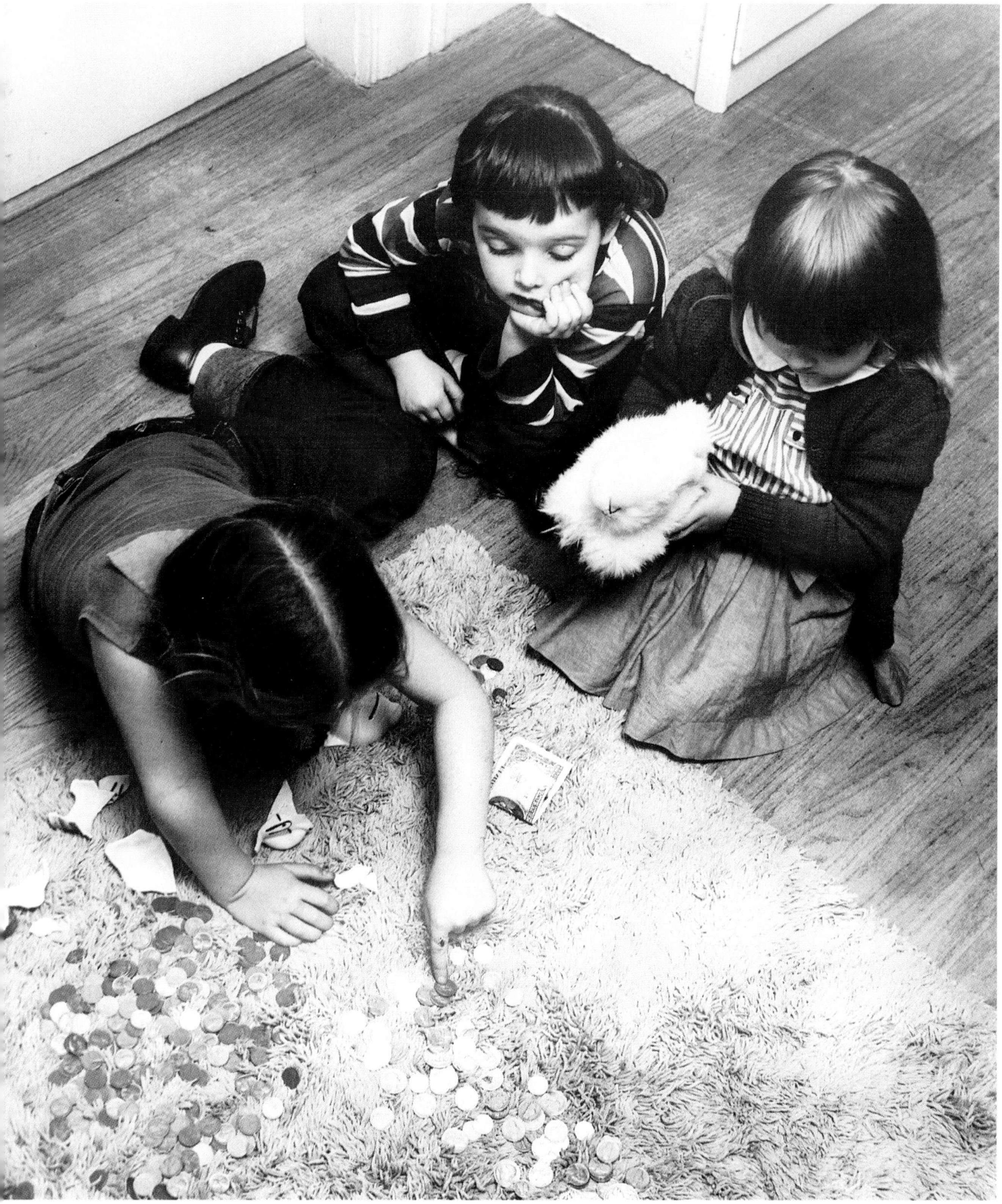

the butterfly
didn't know it was a
butterfly
dreaming it was Chuang Tzu
or Chuang Tzu
dreaming he was a butterfly.
The butterfly never
wondered:
it flew.

OCTAVIO PAZ

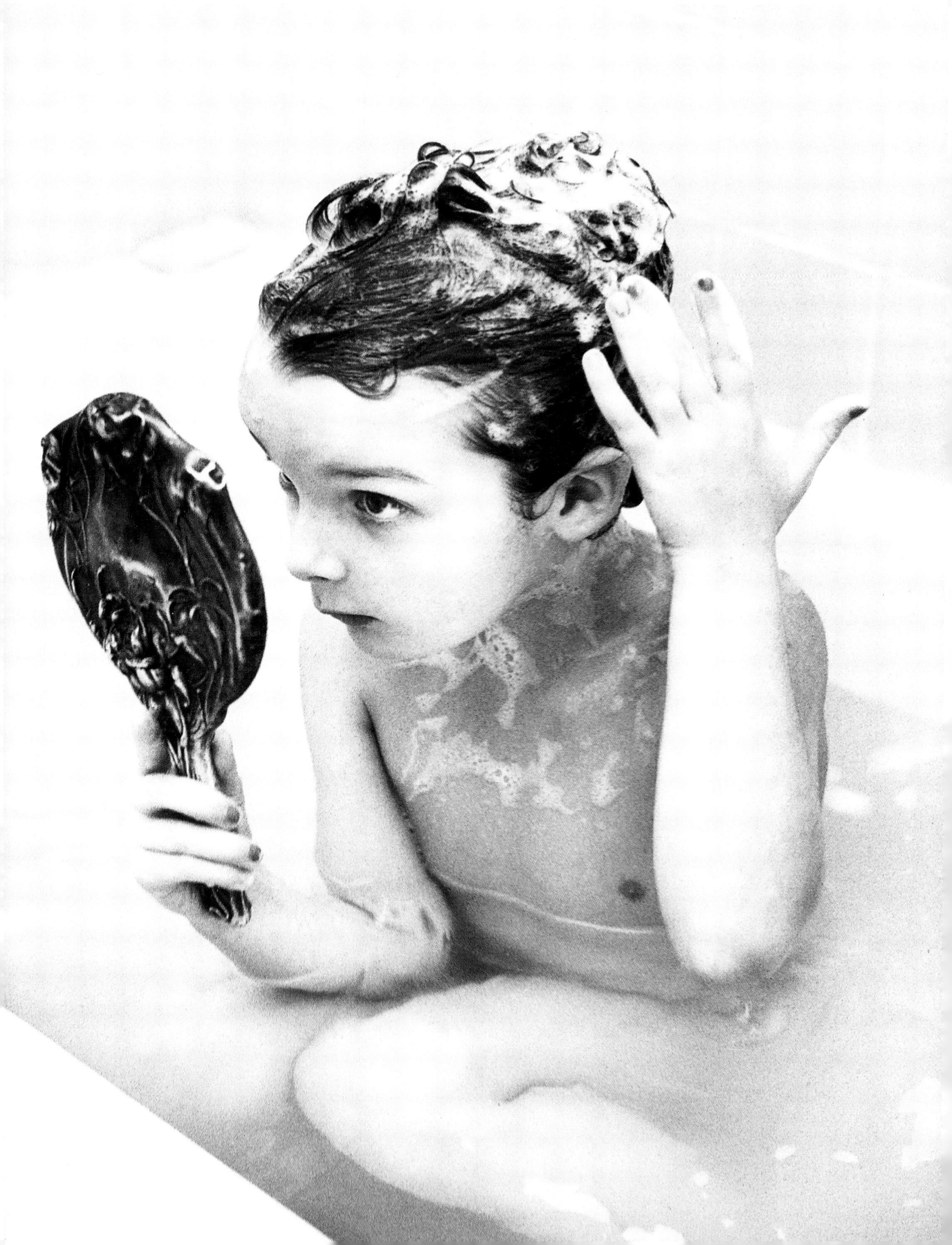

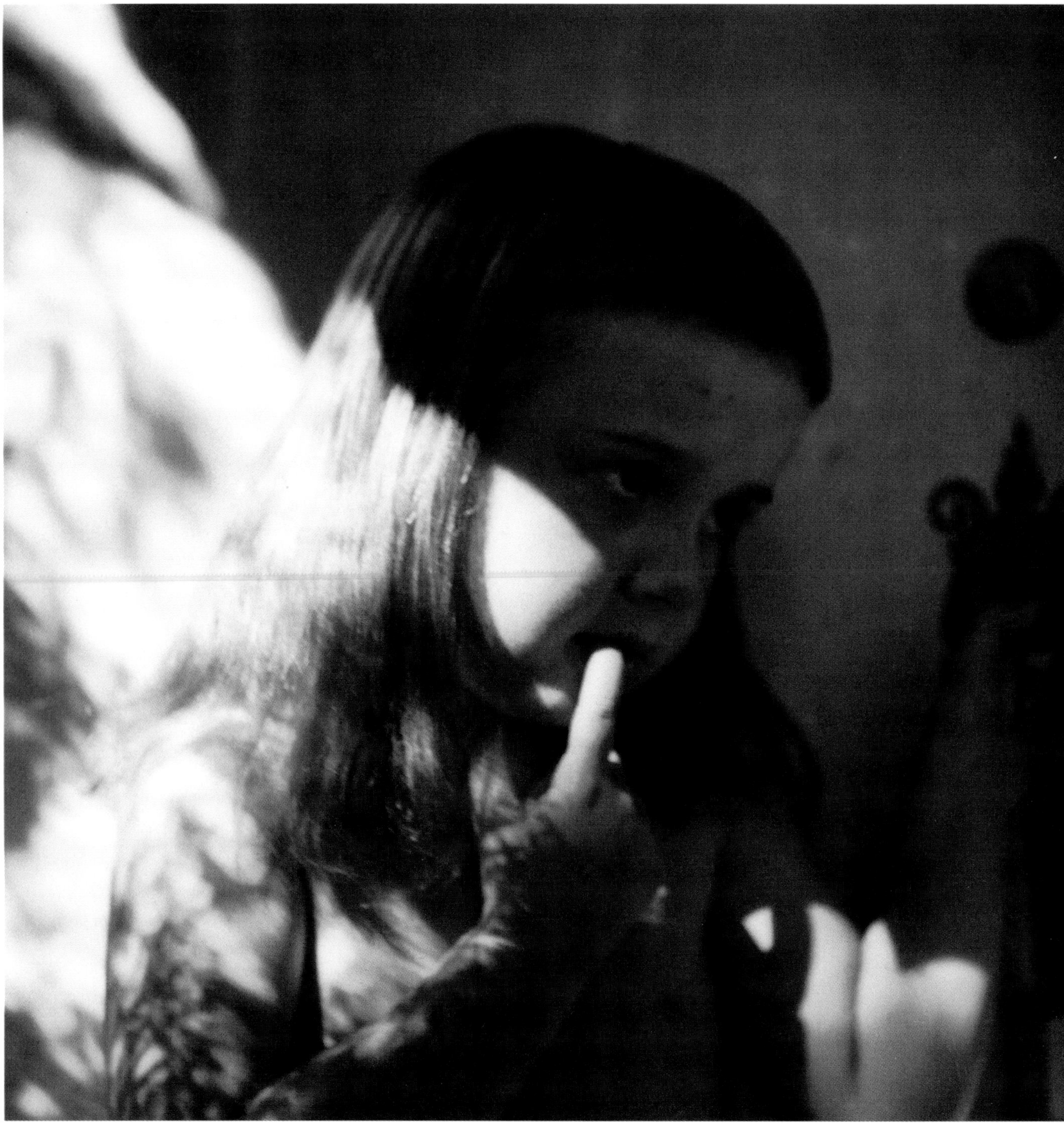

Grief is a Mouse–
And chooses Wainscot in the Breast
For His Shy House–
And baffles quest–

EMILY DICKINSON

Blessed Cecilia, appear in visions
To all musicians, appear and inspire:
Translated Daughter, come down and startle
Composing mortals with immortal fire . . .

W. H. AUDEN

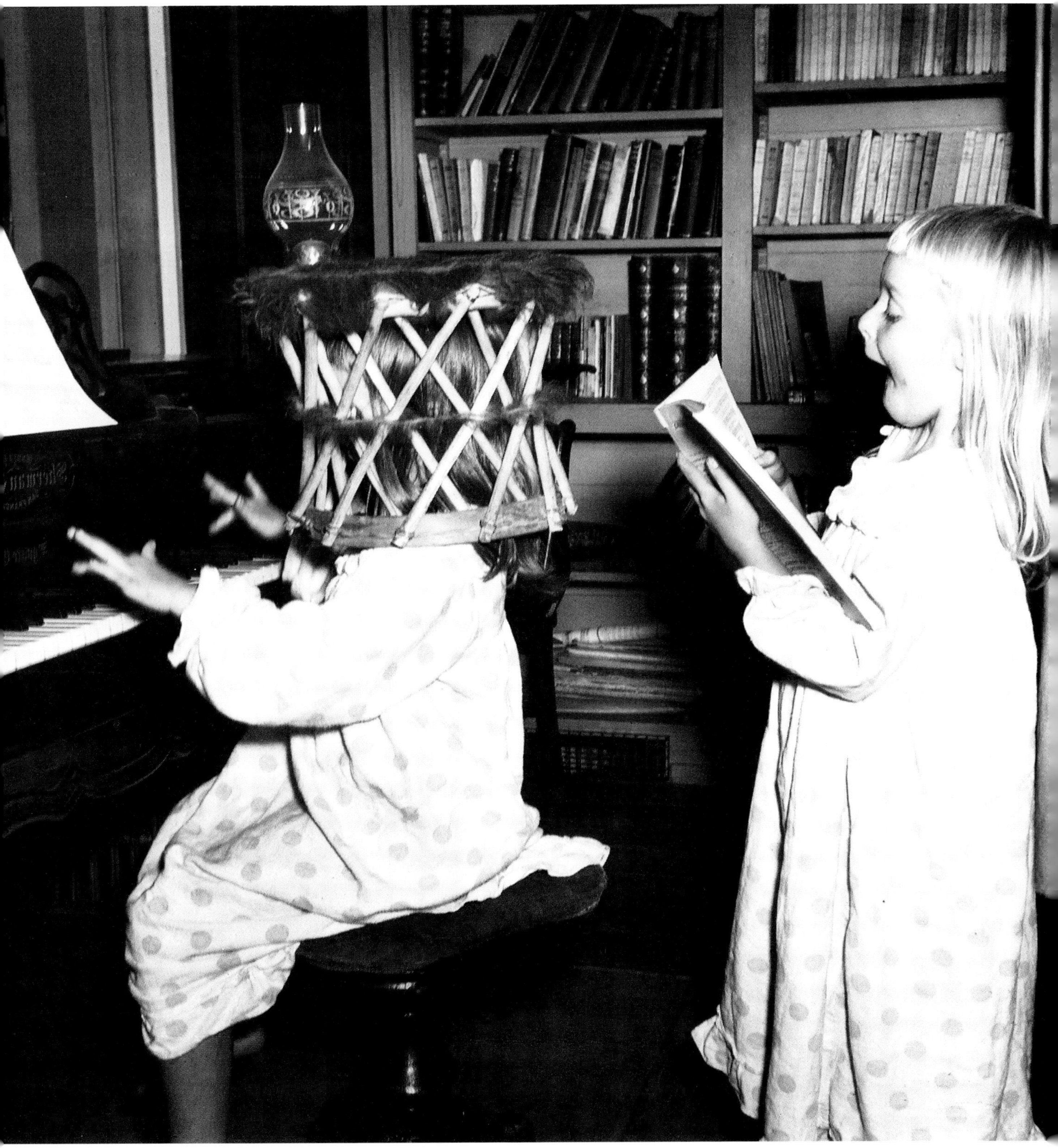

I want to give thanks . . .
For love, which lets us see others
As God sees them.

JORGE LUIS BORGES

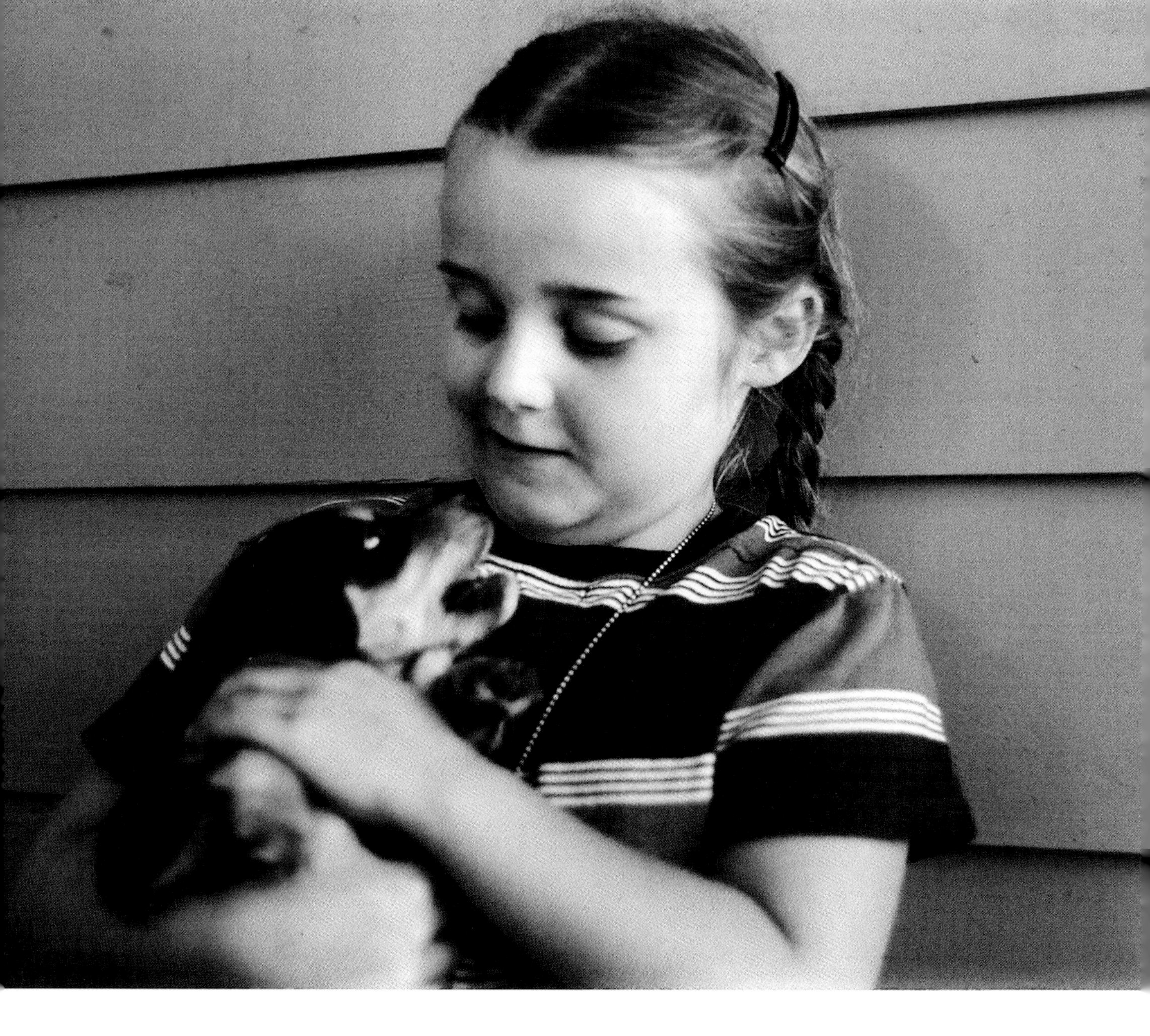

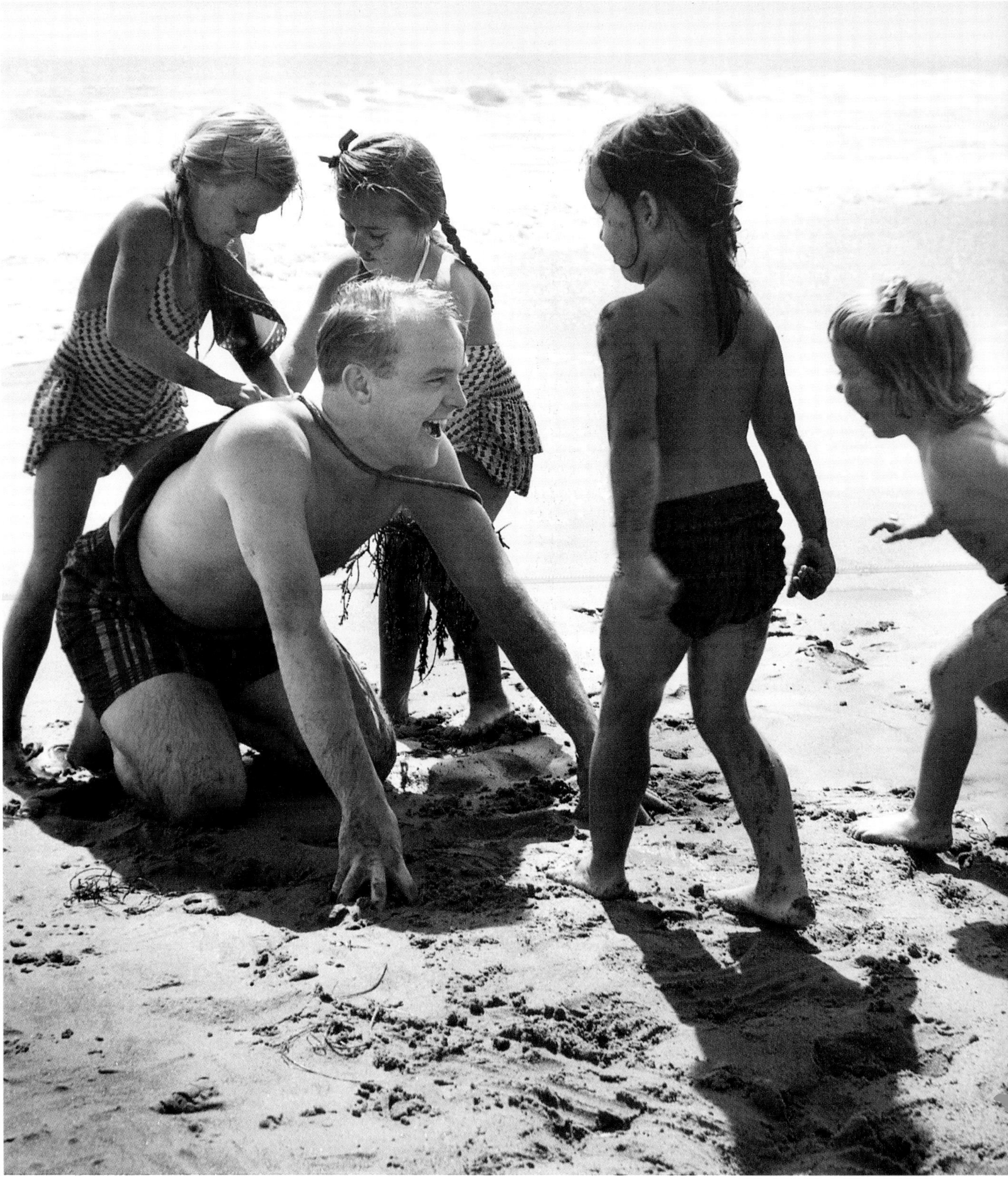

Why should I be surprised
that you have learned
what I have forgotten
and more than I ever knew . . .

RICHARD SHELTON

Come unto these yellow sands

and then take hands:

Curtsied when you have and kiss'd,

The wild waves whist . . .

WILLIAM SHAKESPEARE

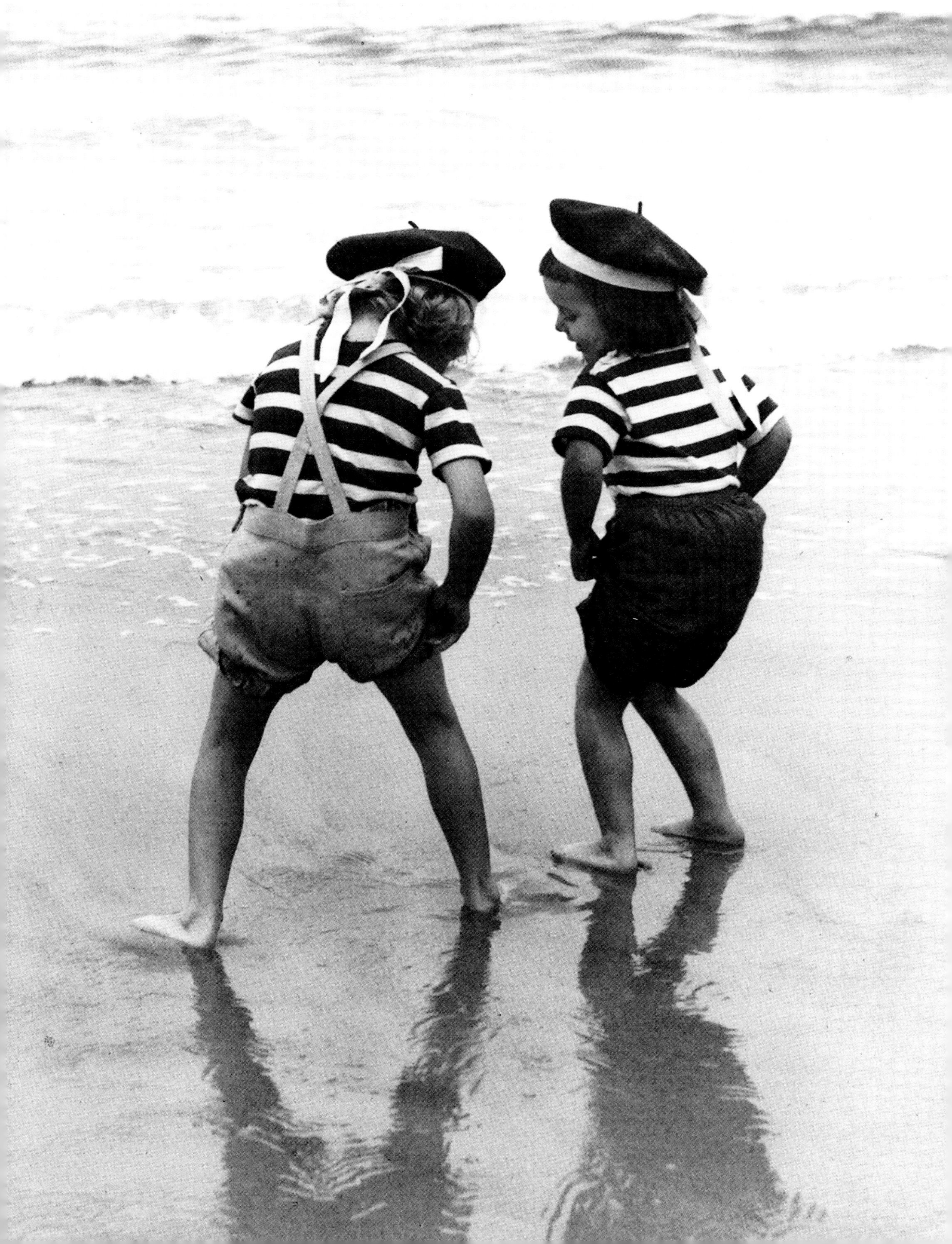

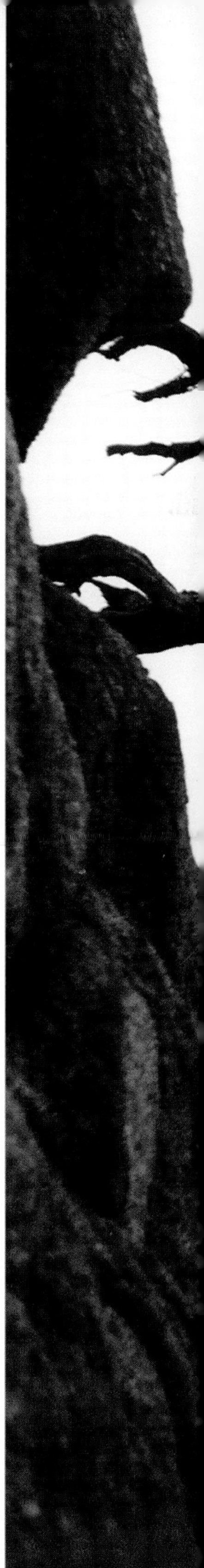

The tree has entered my hands,
The sap has ascended my arms,
The tree has grown in my breast –
Downward,
The branches grow out of me, like arms . . .

EZRA POUND

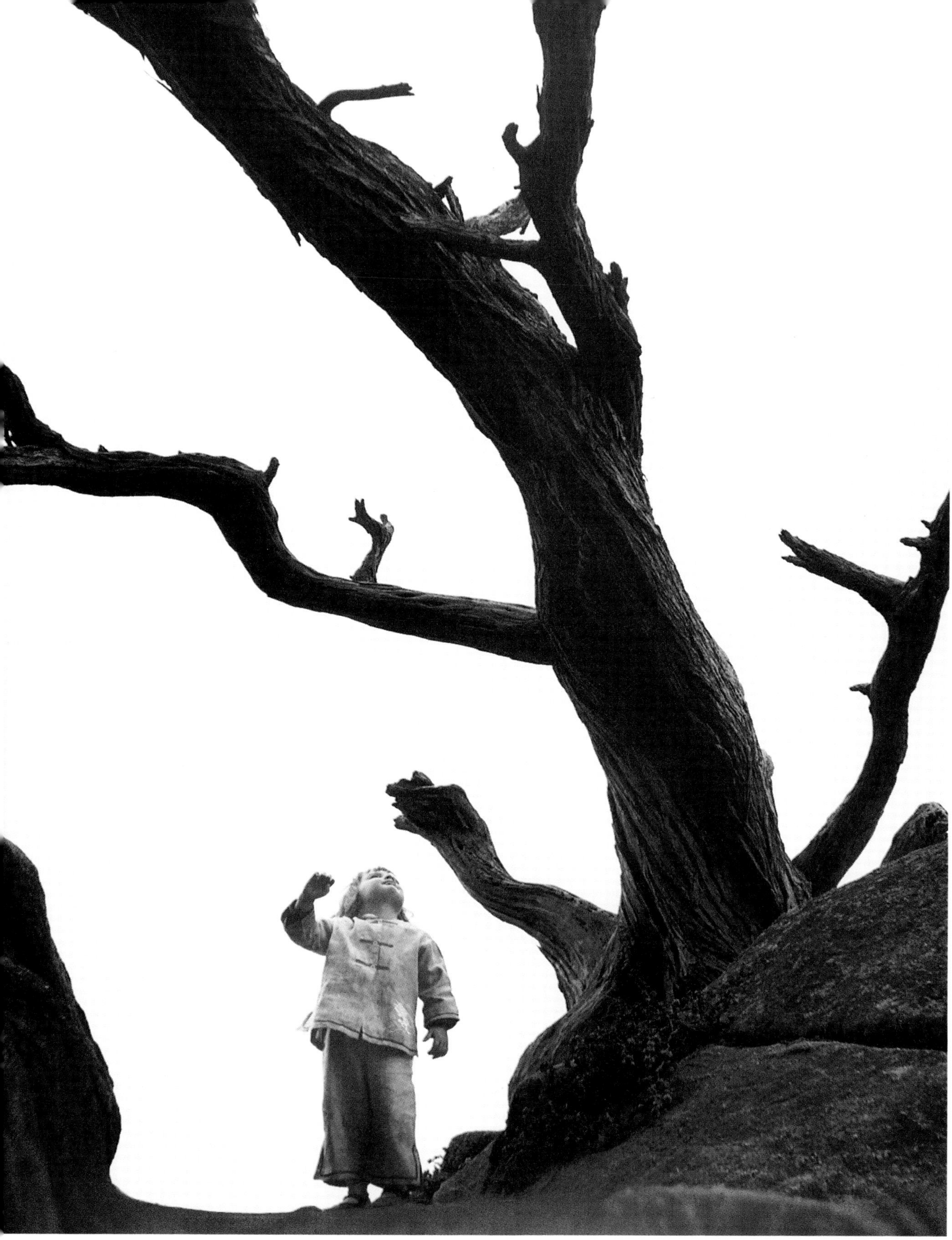

Since ever and ever the world began,

They have danced like a ribbon of flame,

They have sung their song through

the centuries long

And yet it is never the same.

ROSE FYLEMAN

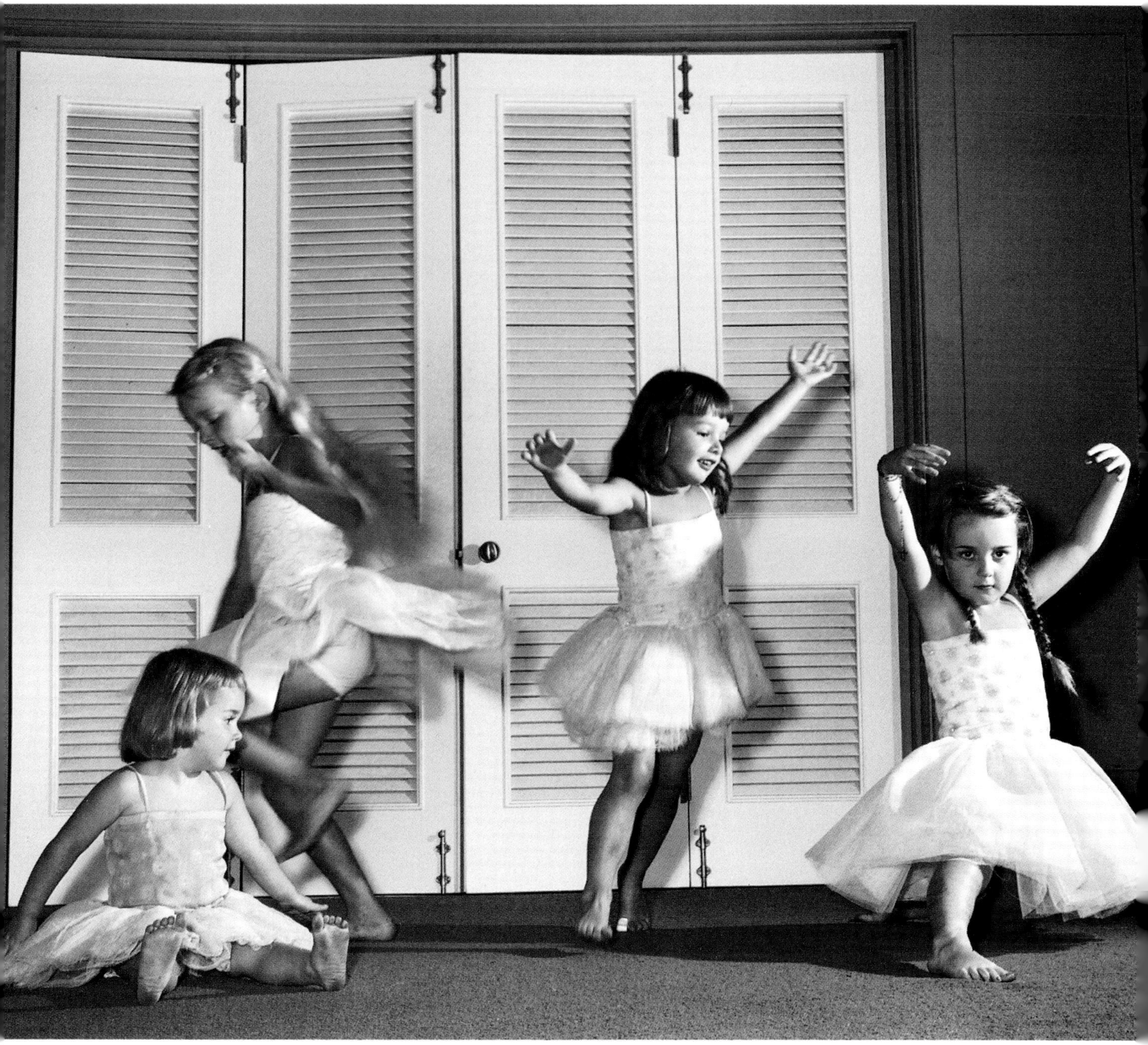

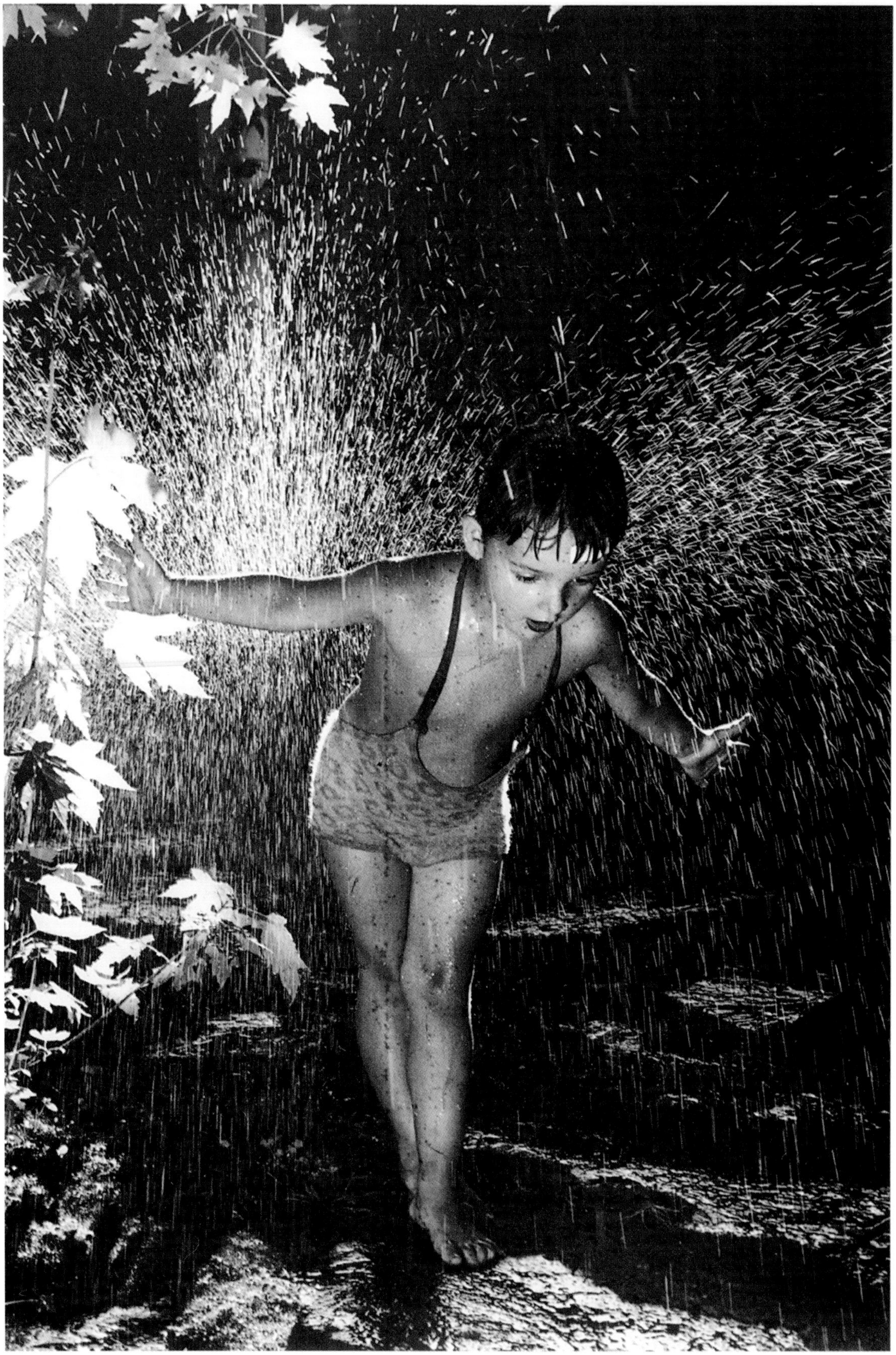

Stillness

not on the branch

in the air

not in the air

in the moment

hummingbird.

OCTAVIO PAZ

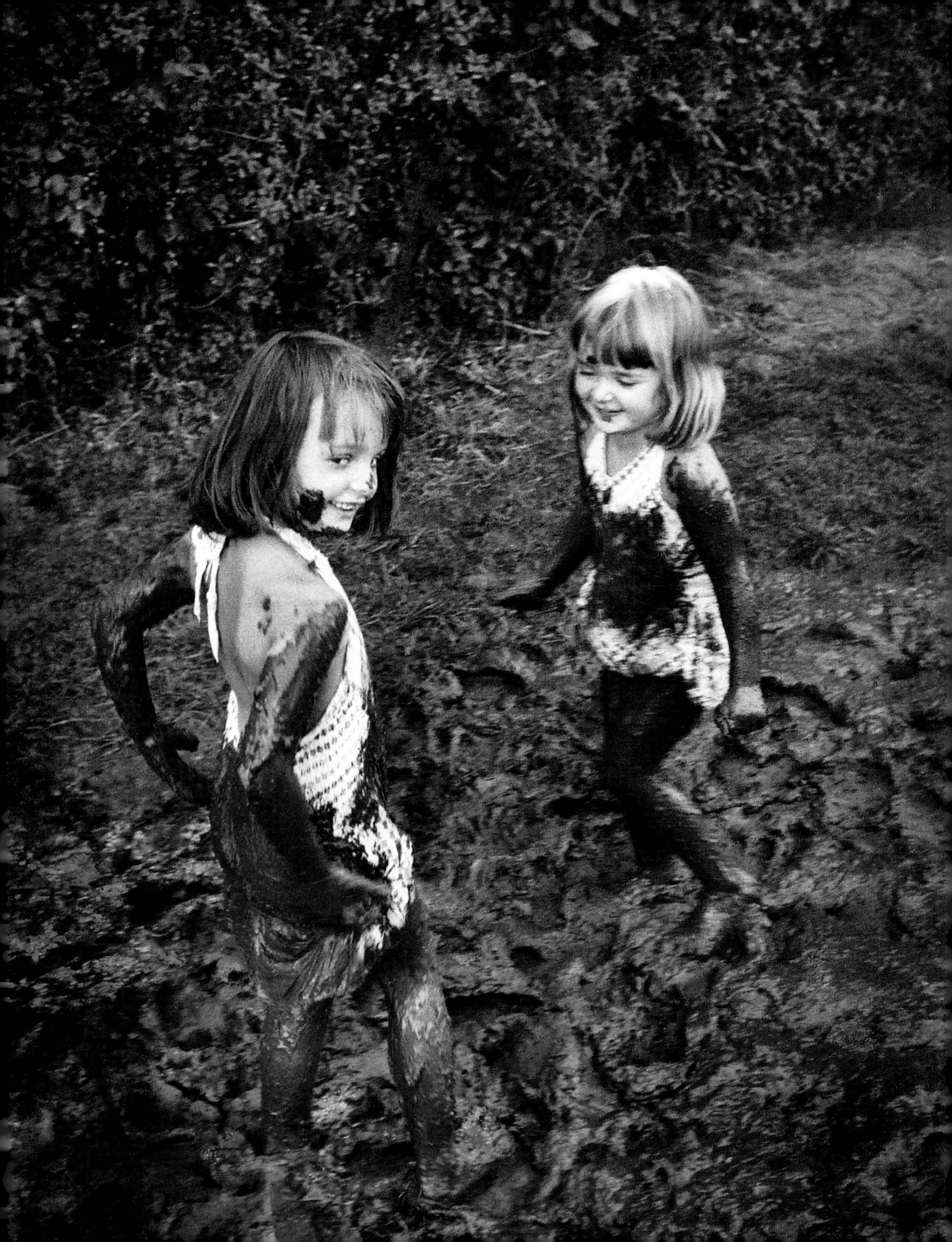

The sun and stars that float in the open air,
The apple-shaped earth and we upon it, surely the drift
of them is something grand,
I do not know what it is except that it is grand, and that
it is happiness.

WALT WHITMAN

What is love? 'Tis not hereafter;
Present mirth hath present laughter;
What's to come is still unsure . . .
Youth's a stuff will not endure.

WILLIAM SHAKESPEARE

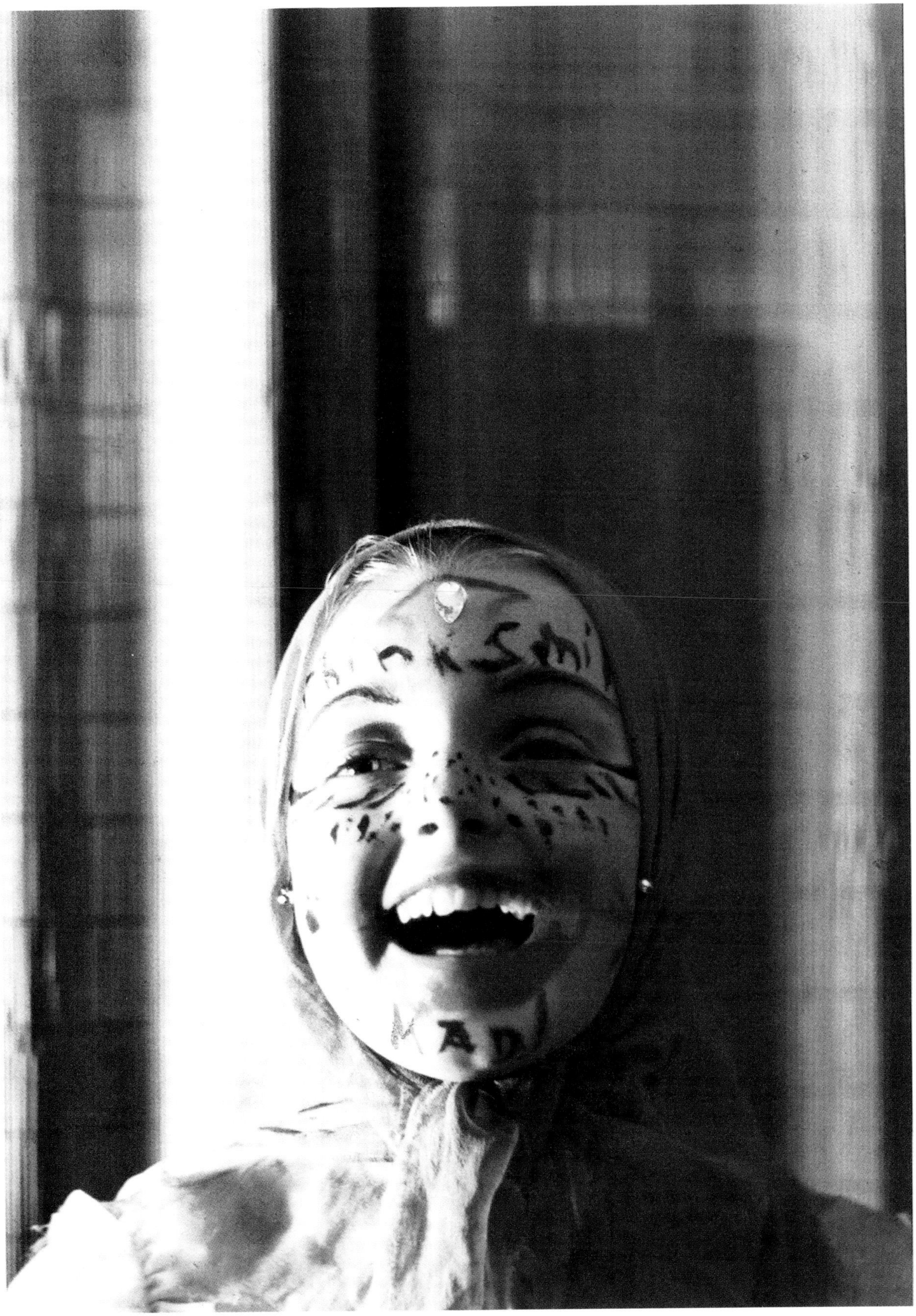

The reality of the other person

is not in what he reveals to you,

but in what he cannot reveal to you.

KAHLIL GIBRAN

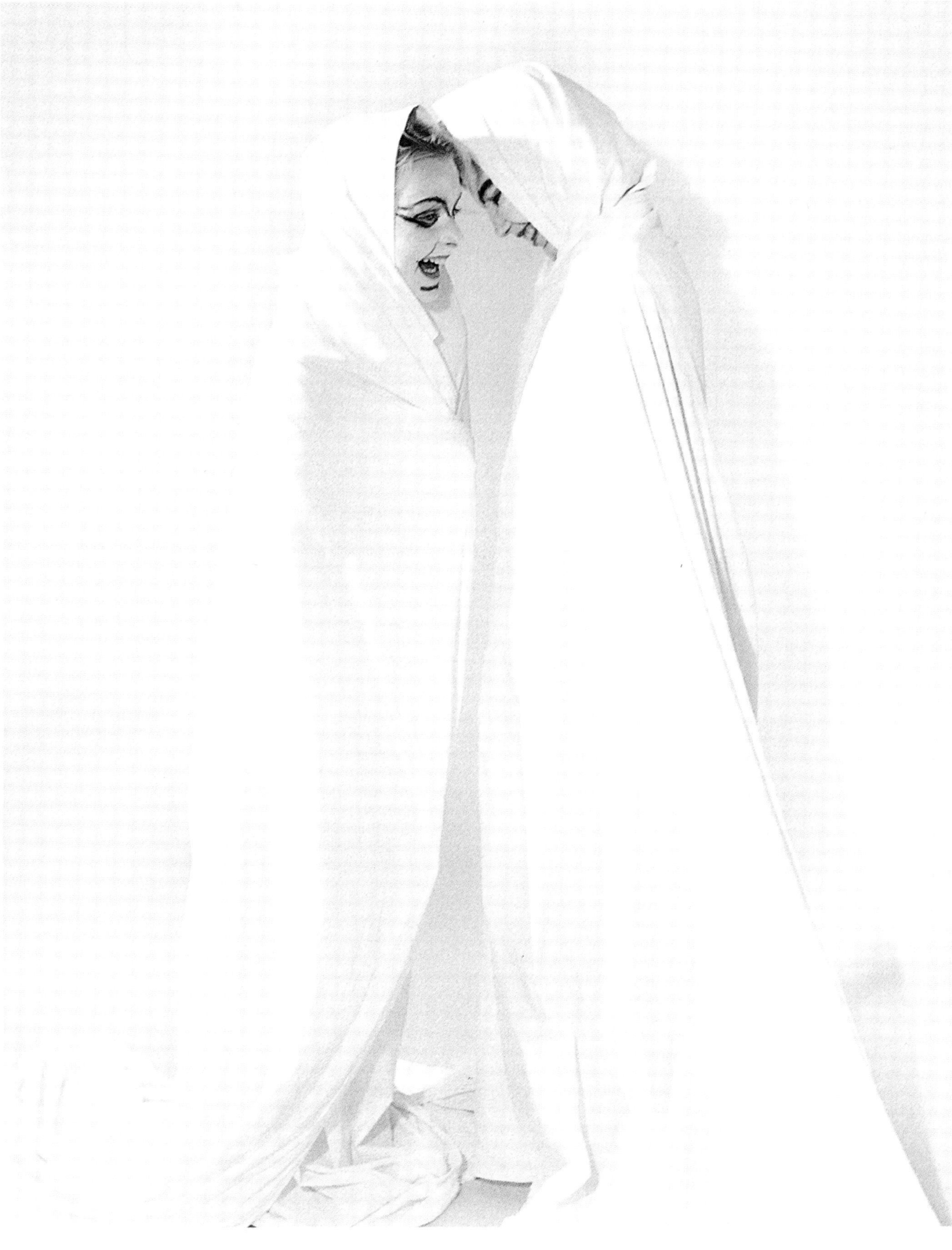

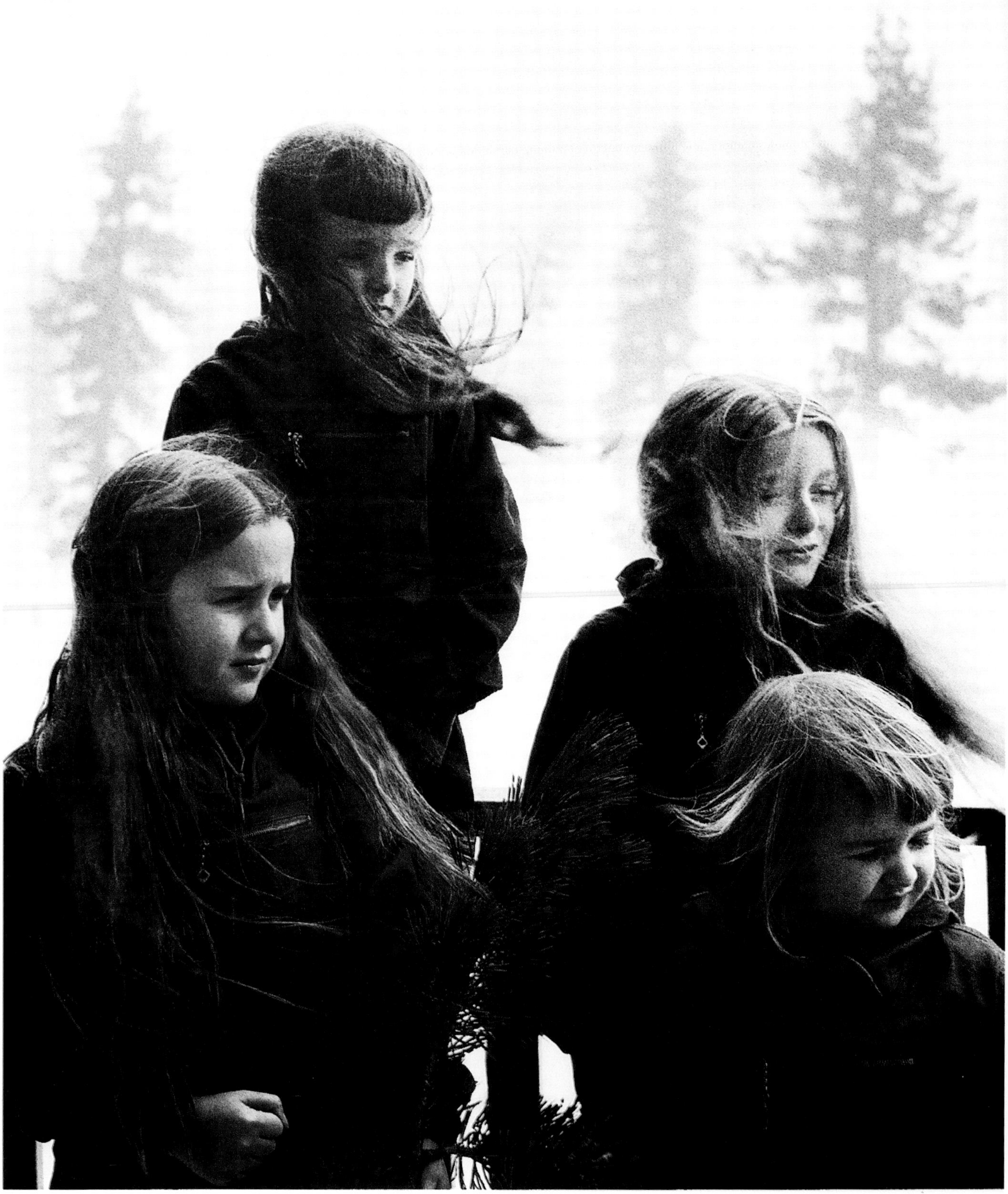

Here we stand in the cold and the sleet,
Blowing fingers and stamping feet,
Come from far away you to greet–
You by the fire and we in the street.

KENNETH GRAHAME

Villagers all, this frosty tide,
Let your doors swing open wide,
Though wind may follow, and snow beside,
Yet draw us in by your fire to bide;
Joy shall be yours in the morning;

KENNETH GRAHAME

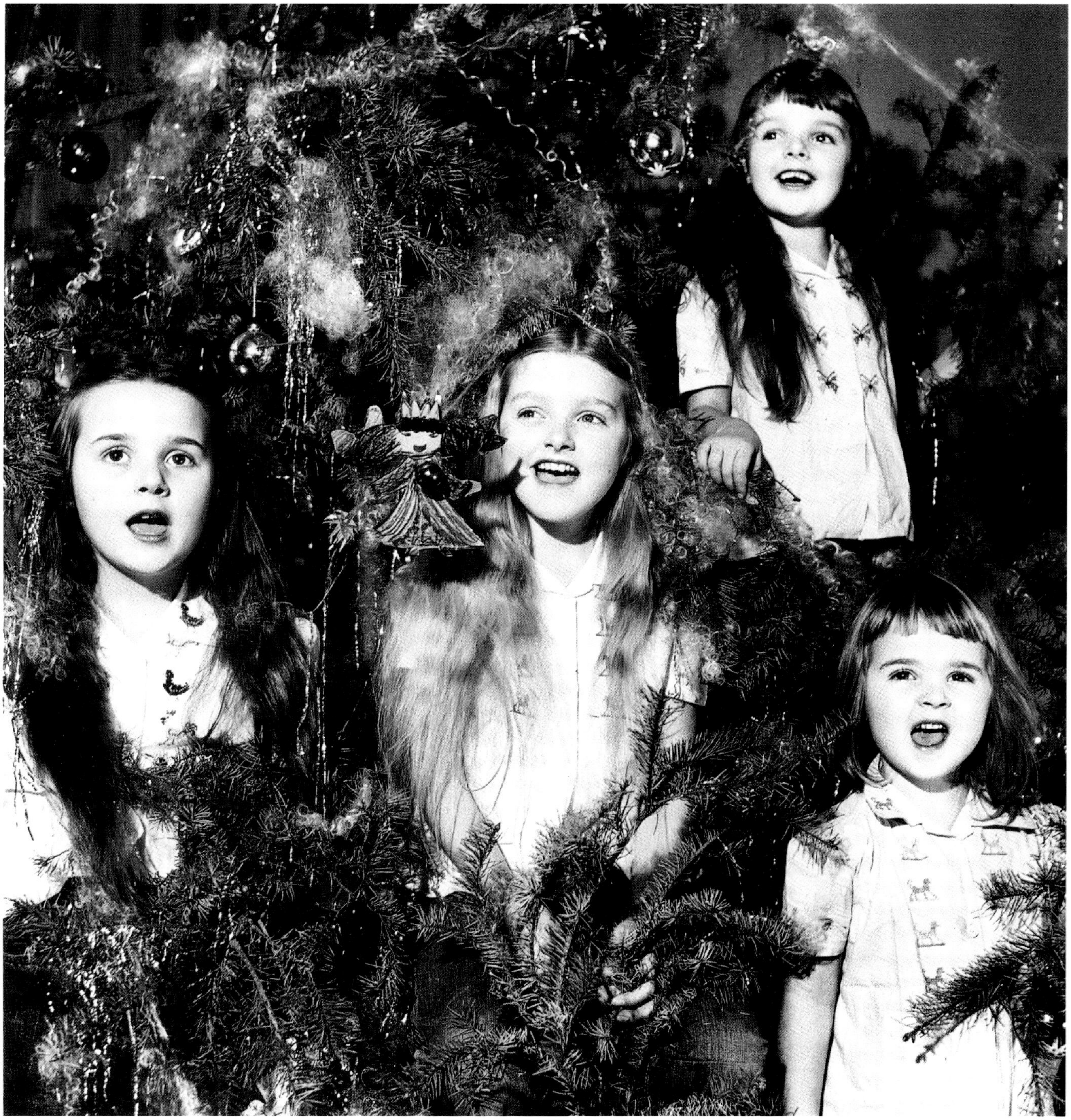

Blossoms will run away,
Cakes reign but a Day.
But Memory like Melody
Is pink Eternally.

EMILY DICKINSON

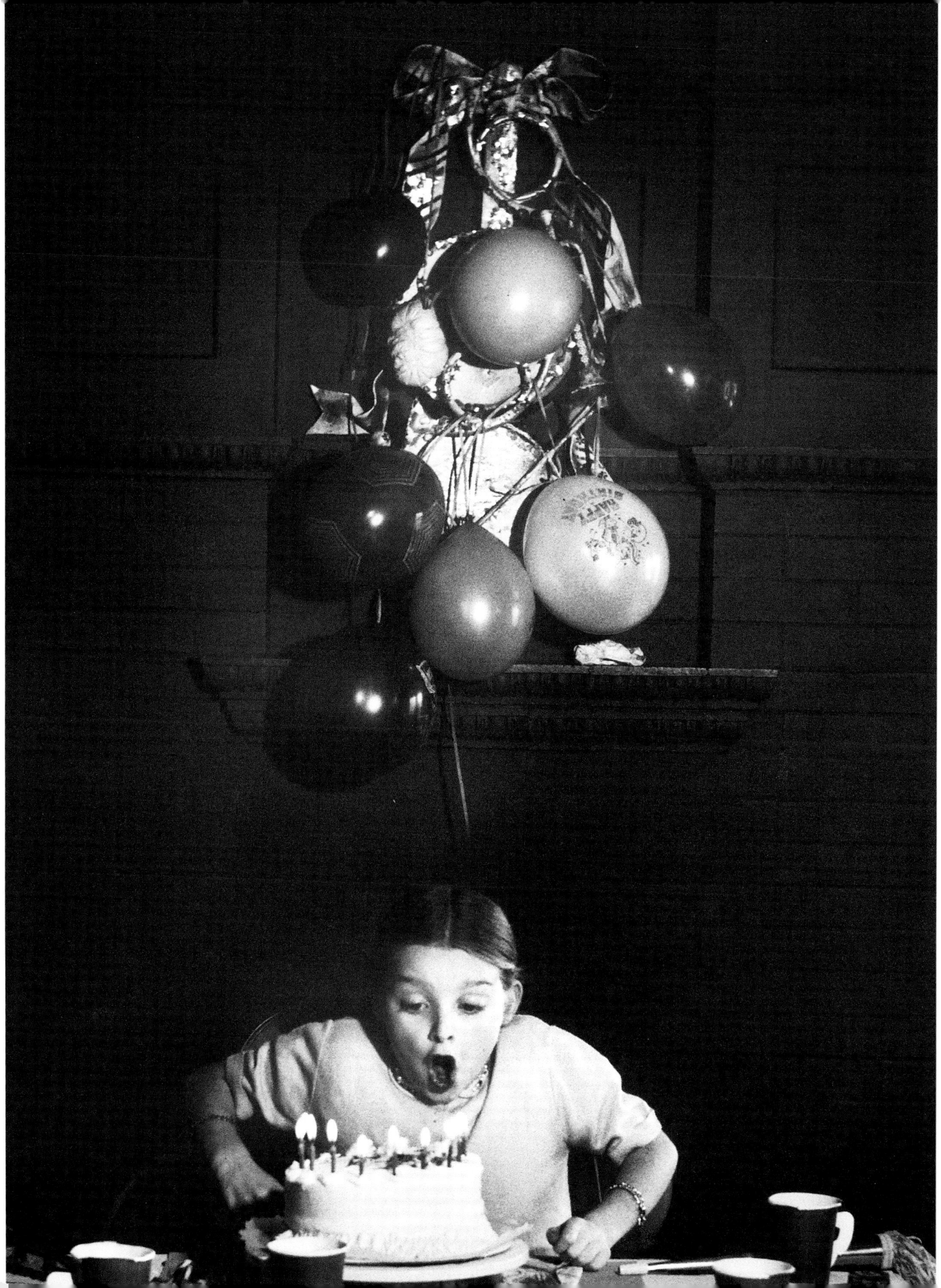

We are friends

My mind and I . . .

Yet sometimes we cannot understand

each other,

As though a cloud had gone over the sun,

Or the pool all blind with trees

Had forgotten the sky.

HILDA CONKLING

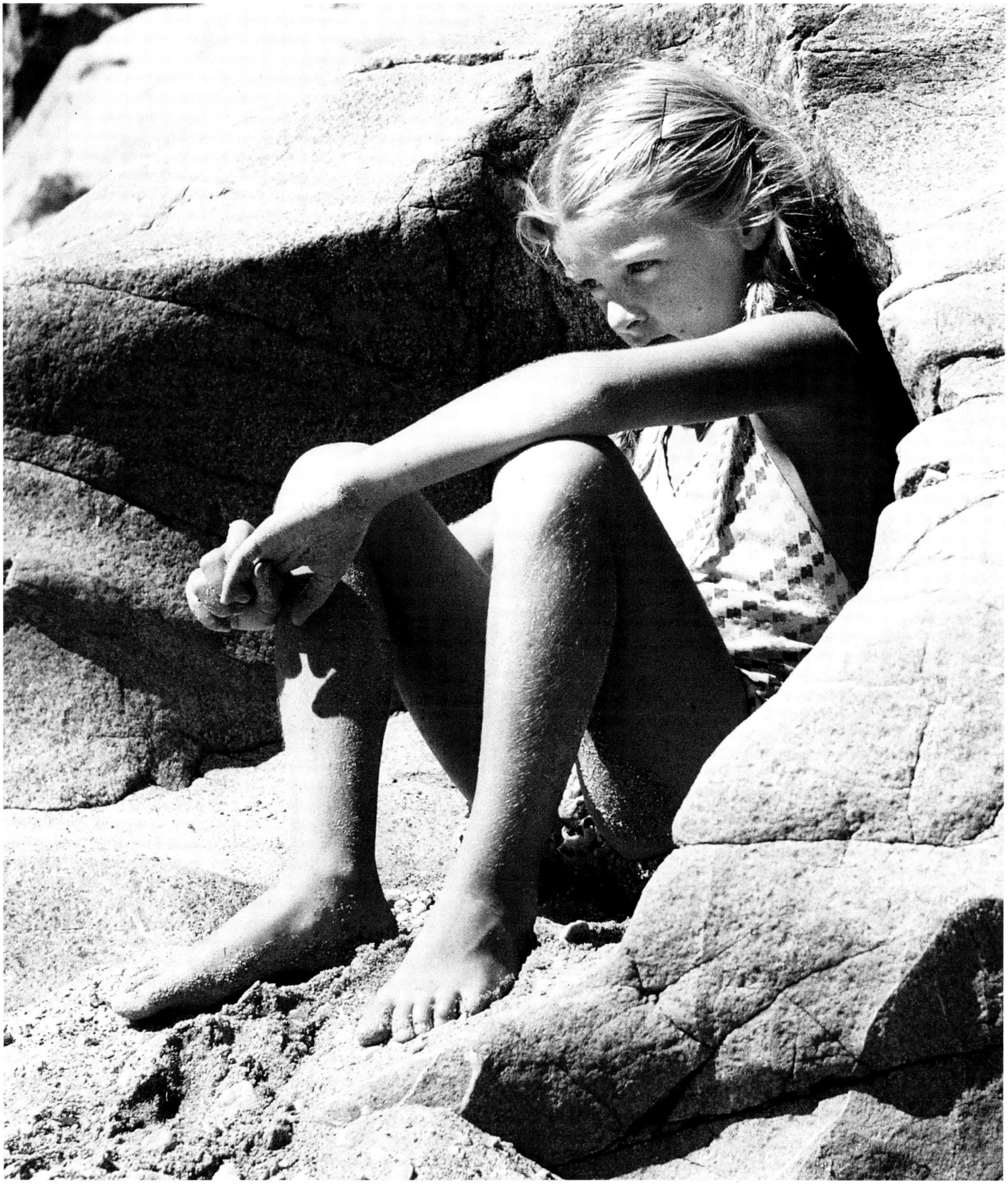

It is as if I always met in those places some grand, serene, immortal, infinitely encouraging, though invisible, companion, and walked with him.

HENRY DAVID THOREAU

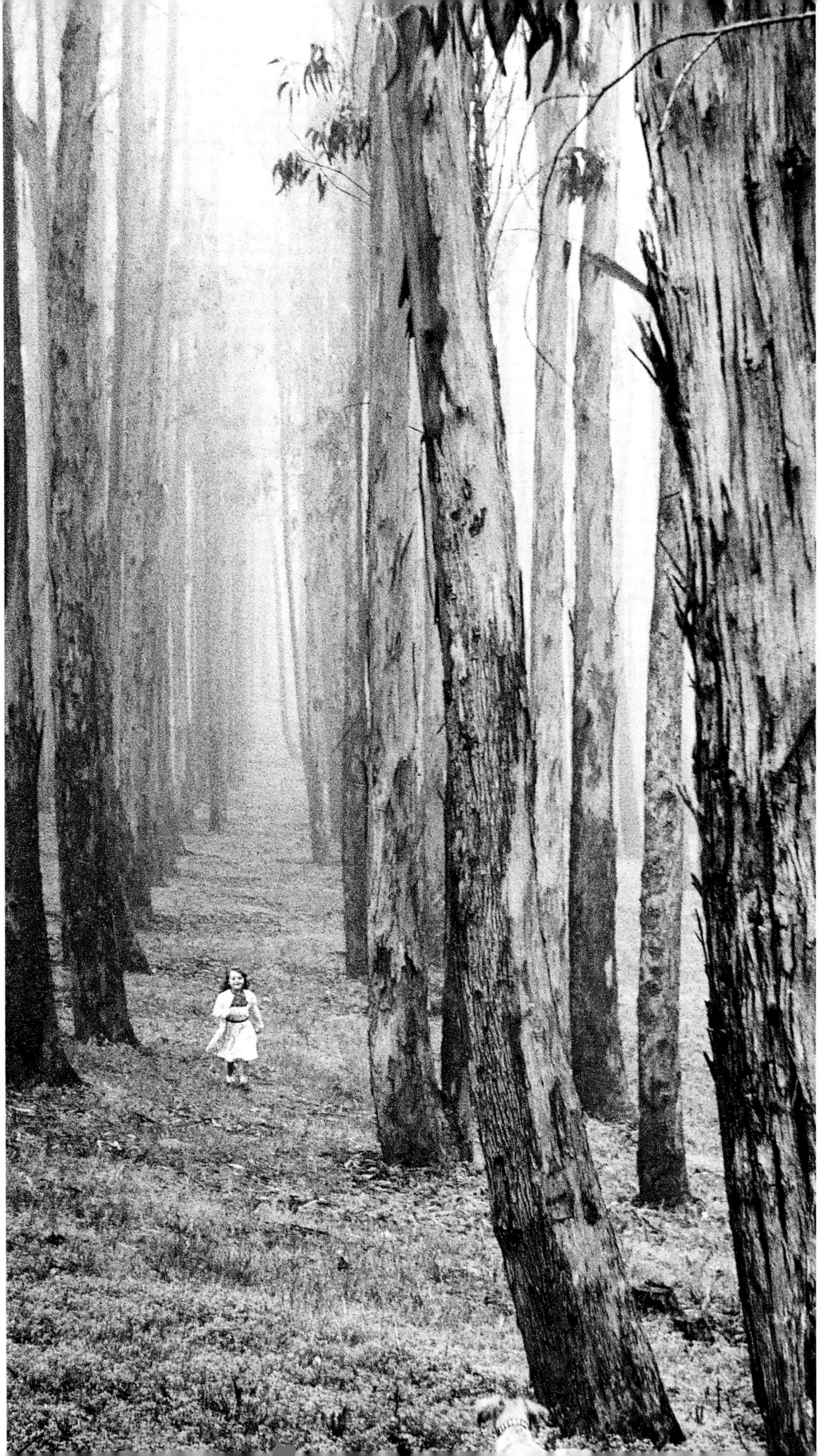

All this stood upon her and was the world
and stood upon her with all its fear and grace . . .
Till in the midst of play,
transfiguring and preparing for the future,
the first white veil descended, gliding softly
over her opened face, almost opaque there,
never to be lifted off again, and somehow
giving to all her questions just one answer:
In you, who were a child once—in you.

RAINER MARIA RILKE

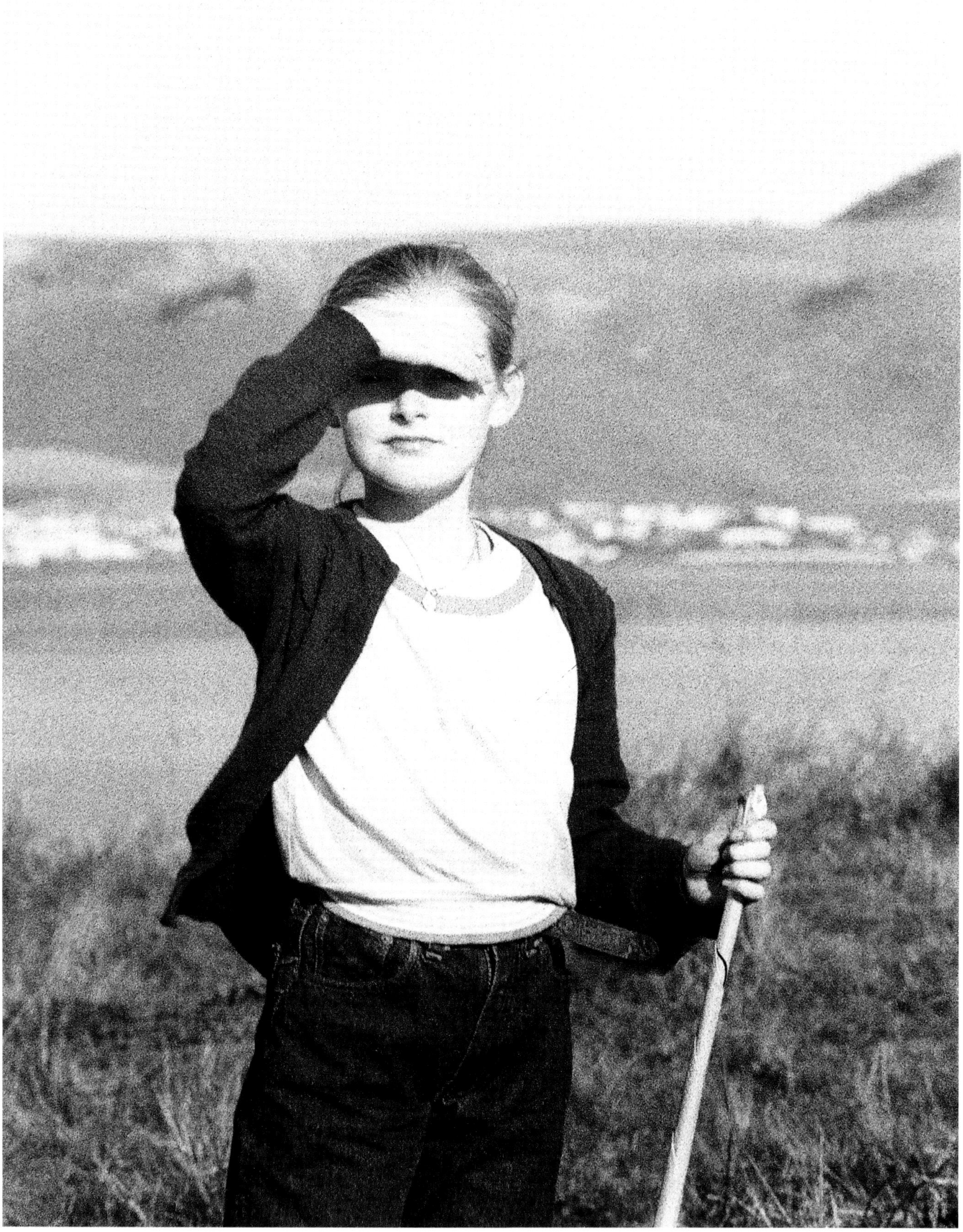

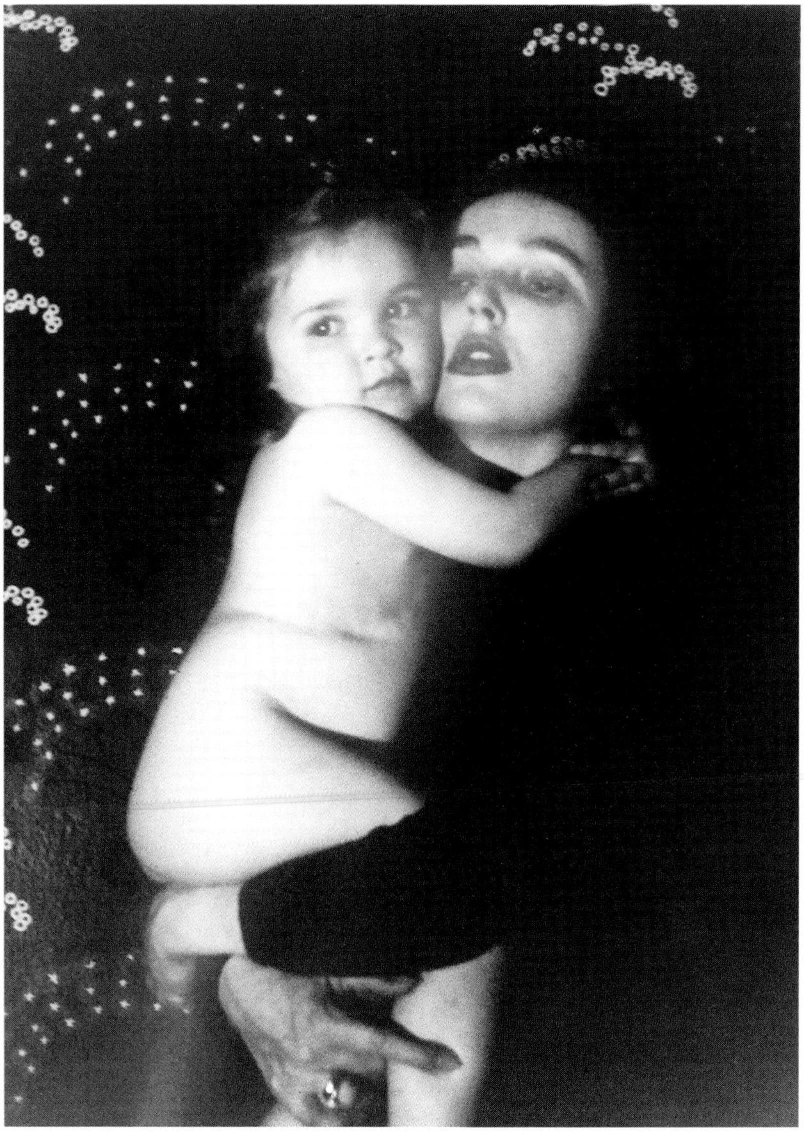

Know the father by deduction,
discovering
from the darkling eyes
of child and mother
what balances remain
to indicate the other.

MYRIAM YOUNG

Acknowledgments

Gratitude to William Alex and Mary Fisher as long as life.
To the indispensable Léa Park and Judy Saldamando for understanding which marks every page.
To photographer Nata Piaskowski for her vision, and to the gifted interpreter and printer, photographer Jason Langer.
To Narcissa Kelley and Burr Overstreet, and to Christiaan, my other self.
To Barbara Johnson, Lucinda Cox, Tina Wahlberg, Mary Wolcott Carlson, Diane Vasica, Jill Scopazzi, Kendal Dodge Butler, Frank Butler, Jane Kastner, Annie Somerville, and my agent Barbara Lucas, who believed, labeled, and launched this performing art in all its versions.
To Steve Ramsey of General Graphics and Saïd Nuseibeh for some beautiful prints.
And first and last, thanks to Gilbert Webb, Peter Volpe, and Stephen Hufford who made the birth possible.

Grateful acknowledgment is made for permission to reproduce excerpts from the following poems:

Borges, Jorge Luis: Excerpt from "Another Poem of Gifts" from *Jorge Luis Borges' Selected Poems 1923–1967*. Copyright © 1968, 1969, 1970, 1971, 1972 by Jorge Luis Borges, Emece Editores, S.A. and Norman Thomas Di Giovanni. Reprinted by permission of Delacorte Press/Seymour Lawrence, a division of Bantam Doubleday Dell Publishing Group, Inc.

Bowra, C. M.: "My heart is all happy" from *Primitive Song.*

Conkling, Hilda: Excerpt from "My Mind and I" from *The New Poetry,* edited by Harriet Monroe and Alice C. Henderson. Published by Macmillan Publishing Company, 1932.

Cummings, E. E.: Excerpt from"May my heart always be open to little" from *Complete Poems: 1904–1962,* edited by George J. Firmage. Reprinted by permission of Liveright Publishing Corporation. Copyright © 1938, 1966, 1991 by the Trustees for the E. E. Cummings Trust.

Gibran, Kahlil: Excerpt from *Sand and Foam.* Published by Alfred A. Knopf, Inc., 1985. Reprinted by permission of Alfred A. Knopf, Inc.

Krishnamurti, Jiddu: Excerpt from *You Are the World.* Copyright © 1972 by Krishnamurti Foundation Trust, Ltd., Brockwood Park, Bramdean, Hampshire, U.K. Reprinted by permission of HarperCollins Publishers, Inc., and Krishnamurti Foundation Trust, Ltd.

Lao-Tzu: Selected lines from # 8 and # 39 from *Tao Te Ching* translated by Stephen Mitchell. Translation copyright ©1988 by Stephen Mitchell. Reprinted by permission of HarperCollins Publishers, Inc.

Lao-Tzu: Selected lines from # 14 from *Tao Te Ching* translated by Gia-fu Feng. Published by Aldershot, Hampshire: Wildwood House, 1973. Reprinted by permission of Alfred A. Knopf, Inc.

Lorca, Federico García: Excerpt from "Balada de la placeta" from *Libro de poemas* translated by Léa C. Park. Translation reprinted by permission of Léa C. Park.

Millay, Edna St. Vincent: Excerpt from "Sonnet XI" of 'Fatal Interview' from *Collected Poems*. Published by Harper Collins Publishers, Inc. Copyright © 1931, 1958 by Edna St. Vincent Millay and Norma Millay Ellis. Reprinted by permission of Elizabeth Barnett, literary executor.

Neruda, Pablo: "Our Child" from *Love Poems of Spain & Spanish America,* edited by Perry Higman. English translation copyright ©1986 by Perry Higman. Reprinted by permission of City Lights Books.

Paz, Octavio: Excerpt from *Octavio Paz: Collected Poems 1952–1987.* Copyright ©1986 by Octavio Paz and Eliot Weinberger. Reprinted by permission of New Directions Publishing Corp.

Pound, Ezra: "A Girl" from *Personae.* Copyright ©1926 by Ezra Pound. Reprinted by permission of New Directions Publishing Corp.

Rilke, Rainer Maria: Excerpt from "The Grownup" from *The Selected Poems of Rainer Maria Rilke.* Copyright ©1982 by Stephen Mitchell. Reprinted by permission of Random House, Inc.

Rilke, Rainer Maria: Excerpt from "The Book of Pictures II.1" reprinted from *Translations from the Poetry of Rainer Maria Rilke.* Translated from the German by M. D. Herter Norton, with the permission of W. W. Norton & Company, Inc. Copyright ©1938 by W. W. Norton & Company, Inc., renewed ©1966 by M. D. Herter Norton.

Rilke, Rainer Maria: Excerpt from # 4 reprinted from *Sonnets to Orpheus.* Translated from the German by M. D. Herter Norton, with the permission of W. W. Norton & Company, Inc. Copyright © 1942 by W. W. Norton & Company, Inc., renewed ©1970 by M. D. Herter Norton.

Shelton, Richard: Excerpt from "Letting Go" from *Selected Poems, 1969–1981*, copyright © 1982. Reprinted by permission of the University of Pittsburgh Press.

Thomas, Dylan: Excerpt from *A Child's Christmas in Wales.* Copyright ©1952 by Dylan Thomas. Reprinted by permission of New Directions Publishing Corp.

Young, Myriam: "Striped shirts at seashore" reprinted courtesy of Eastman Kodak Company.